HOW TO CREATE
NEW IDEAS

Every man who knows how to read has it in his power to magnify himself, to multiply the ways in which he exists, to make his life full, significant and interesting.

—ALDOUS HUXLEY

HOW TO CREATE

NEW IDEAS

More Than a Book—
A Comprehensive Course in
THE ART AND SCIENCE
OF CREATIVE THINKING

by

Jack W. Taylor

Director of Management Development
Packaging Corporation of America

Englewood Cliffs, N.J.
PRENTICE-HALL, INC.

PRINTED IN THE UNITED STATES OF AMERICA
40446—M O

To

CLOYD S. STEINMETZ,
who first made me so uncomfortable
with my comfortable ideas
that I vowed I'd show him—
only to discover that
he had shown me a great teacher's creative love

and

JAMES C. MORRIS,
who has constantly encouraged me to do
what has needed to be done
with my ideas,
and has shown me a great executive's creative love.

BEFORE YOU START...

Here are ten things you may find it helpful to know:

1. This is not a book about painting masterpieces, inventing solar-powered space ships, making a million dollars, or building widgets, gimmicks or gadgets. (Even if I knew anything about these things—which I don't—they still would not constitute the focal point of this effort.) It is a book about *the mental processes* that underlie such creative feats—and may lead to them if one is so motivated.

2. It does no good to advise anyone to "Think," or "Use your imagination," and stop there. Such advice, however well-intentioned, leaves the advisee at a frustrated loss, for it fails to explain *how*. My purpose here is to avoid this deficiency and, instead, to concentrate upon the job of explaining some of the most significant things known about *how to think creatively*.

3. This book is meant to be different. Not different just because that is in keeping with the essential nature of Creative Thinking. Not different for mere difference's sake. Different for the sake of usefulness, betterness, clarity, completeness, interest, and easiness—for you.

4. The notion persists popularly that creative ability is some strange, mysterious, esoteric faculty—an almost magical faculty possessed exclusively by the blessed, chosen few. ("Either you have it, or you don't.") I, for one, don't believe it. On the contrary, I am convinced that . . .
    Every human being has some creative ability—most of it latent.

vii

Every person can raise the level of creativity at which he
has been habitually functioning.

The origination of ideas can be almost as definite a process
as the production of material things.

In generating new ideas, the creative mind follows operating procedures that can be learned and controlled.

And I aim to prove these convictions to your satisfaction and
benefit.

5. This book derived from more than two decades of tedious
but continuing study of creativity via . . .

Investigation of published reports on scientific research
in this and related fields.

Study of general psychology, logic, philosophy, science, *et al.*

Analysis of my own habitual mental processes—good and
bad.

Discussions with successful innovators in various fields of
endeavor.

Study of written case histories of creative people, their
accomplishments, and their methods.

Observation of, and participation with, creative people at
work.

Experimentation with individuals, formal adult classes in
The Art of Creative Thinking, and creative groups
"in workshop".

Point: The principles and methods described in this book
have been tested.

They work.

6. There are no slick, quick, trick short-cuts to creativity
here. If there are any such in existence—anywhere—I haven't
been able to find them. Rather, the choices seem to be only
between using sound principles or not-so-sound, and good
methods or not-so-good. The good and sound make the task
easier, but let no one be fooled: Creative Thinking is hard work.
(Only men, not boys, need apply.)

7. It costs much to boot-strap one's creativity. But it is worth
more than it costs.

8. The attitudes you bring to the study of Creative Thinking are pivotally important. If, for instance, you are determined to cling to all previous conceptions of "Experienced Judgment" or "Common Sense", you will be off to a flying bad start. Experienced Judgment *may* be infinitely experienced and judicious, as inferred. Common Sense *may* be uncommonly sensible, as implied. The creative mind is skeptical, though: it underlines the "may's" and goes on to investigate.

9. Big, technical-sounding, obscure words and terms arouse my suspicions. Too often, I have found, they are used for displays of erudition—or as watchdogs to keep intruders out of "private" domains—or as semantical smoke screens. (For example, I once asked a psychologist why it was such a thrill to ride a roller coaster. "Kinesthesia," he said. I looked this up and found it was a Greek word meaning "sense of motion". Thus the "explanation" explained no more in Greek than in English.) On the hunch that you feel somewhat as I do about words of this kind, I have avoided using them in this book except where they serve some constructive purpose. If they are not explained at the point of use, where used, it is because they are probably not very important.

10. The term, "Creative Thinking," is quite a mouthful. Hereinafter, for the most part, I will shorten it to CT. This will save time and effort for everyone.

J.W.T.

WHAT'S IN THIS BOOK?

HOW TO CREATE
NEW IDEAS

First

WHAT'S THIS ALL ABOUT?

Look around you. What do you see? Metal, wood, plastics, paper, paint?

Look around again—from a different vantage point. What do you see this time? Machines, buildings, tools, books, pictures?

Once more—look again—from still another point. Now what do you see? *Ideas?* Ideas that transformed old, familiar things into new things—new things of utility, safety, beauty? Ideas that produced greater efficiency, pleasure, security, comfort, spirituality, leisure, health?

The day that you have fixed the regular habit of looking at things in this third fashion will be the day that you have really begun to be a highly creative person.

In truth, this Third Look is very nearly a definition of CT. If you would like a more formal definition, here is the one that I prefer:

> *Creative Thinking is the development of new ideas which will satisfy some expressed or implied need of mankind.*

That's what this is all about.

"Who—Me?"

"Well, that leaves me out. Why, *I* could never write a *Crime and Punishment,* or develop a polio vaccine, or compose a *Fifth Symphony,* or invent a rocket motor, or conceive a *Theory of Relativity,* or design a UN Building, or win a Nobel Prize, or anything like that!"

Is this what you have just said, or are saying, to yourself? If

1

so, all right; so be it. Perhaps you are *not* another Tolstoy, or Salk, or Beethoven, or Einstein, or who-have-you. And quite possibly you may never create a planet-rocking innovation, no matter how much you might wish to do so.

(How will you ever find out whether you can or cannot, by the way?)

But hold on a moment! You may be jumping to a misconception, and missing the point about CT altogether.

There is nothing whatever in the definition of CT which either explicitly or implicitly connotes that a globe-rattling idea is one whit more creative than one having a relatively tiny sphere of impact. Size has nothing to do with it, really. An idea for a new pin is just as creative as an idea for a cyclotron!

Further—as though you hadn't already noticed—there is considerable evidence that the world doesn't even *want* a constant stream, mass or succession of great, revolutionary, high-powered, magnificent, overwhelming, earth-shattering ideas. (Hasn't it struck you as just a little odd, for example, that after all these years we still have comprehended the Christian Idea only as a theory, and not as a practice?) On the contrary, it seems apparent that our insatiable global appetite for new ideas is on a somewhat more mundane level: leaky faucets, job output, the children's lessons, pay raises, letters, tools, recreation, cooking, classified ads, highway markers, glare. . . . These and countless thousands of other kindred elements of our workaday life are no less demanding of the attention of creative minds. And if this is where you feel most at home, fine!—for this, too, is the "proper" realm of CT; and even the most modest contribution made on this plane may also move the world measurably and desirably forward.

Creative Thinking is the development of new ideas—of *whatever* magnitude, on *every* plane, in *any* field of human interest and endeavor—which will satisfy some expressed or implied need or needs of mankind. So . . .

"Who, me," you say? *Certainly,* you! You, of *all* people. And *that's* what this is all about.

Second

HOW DO WE GET IT?

The essence of Creative Thinking is contained in the word "new."* This word further connotes: *different, original, uncommon, unique, unusual.*

The end purpose of CT is to *do* something new and different; *think up* something new and different; *produce* new, different, unique, unusual, ingenious, original *ideas*—ideas that will satisfy some expressed or implied need or needs of mankind.

The instrument with which we can accomplish this—the human brain— is not very big. It weighs only about three pounds. But it is the most powerful machine on earth!

In a simplified but important sense, each of us really has *three* brains:

1. *The Retainer.* This is the "storehouse," the memorizer. It saves up experience, knowledge—information—for use by the other two brains. Research shows that we tend to forget about 90 per cent of what we learn during a lifetime. Yet, at maturity, our Retainer is estimated to contain *ten times* as much information as the nine million volumes in the Library of Congress! The Retainer is useful to CT, of course, but not in the way many people seem to believe. Many who believe that they are thinking creatively actually are merely *remembering* what they have encountered in the past and temporarily forgotten—or what someone else has thought up and conveyed to them.

*"New" means new to *you,* regardless of whether you, alone, or you-plus-100-others, happened to think of an idea first. Primacy is beside the point, for our purposes here. If an idea occurs to you that has never before occurred to you, that idea—to you—is new.

3

2. *The Analyzer*. This is the "sizer-upper," the judge. It appraises, weighs, evaluates, and makes decisions. This brain, too, is useful to CT—when applied in the right way at the right time. Frequently, however, it is so over-developed, dominant, misapplied and misused that it completely *blocks* CT. (More about this later.)

3. *The Imaginer*. This is the "thinker-upper," the generator of new ideas.

Each of these brains is important, not only to successful CT, but to an individual's very, satisfactory functioning in life. And, as we go along, I hope to provide you with definite aids to finding better, more rewarding ways to use each one. But the one on whose use I am going to concentrate the most is the *Imaginer*, because (1) *it is both the least used and the least understood of the three*, and (2) *its use provides by far the greatest benefits*.

If you doubt the first of the two statements, just above, try this:
> Make a list of all the *new ideas* you have produced during the past year.
> Make a list of all the *judgments* or analyses or decisions you have made during the past year—if possible.
> Make a list of all the *recollections* you have had during the past year—if you can.
> Compare your three lists and check: Which one contains the greatest number of items?

If you doubt the second of the above statements, try this:
> Make a list of the first ten useful objects you see.
> Make a list of the ten things, tangible or otherwise, that you value most in life.
> Check the *origin* of the items on both lists.
> Ponder this statement: "Ideas are the beginning of everything that man wants from life."

What say, now?

Where Shall We Start?

How shall we start on the job of finding out where and how to get this so-desirable thing, CT ability?

Rather than try to answer this question in words alone—which would impose upon you a mere passive role—I am going to ask you presently to carry out two exercises which will not only enable you to play an active and interesting role, but which will vivify the answers and make them much more meaningful for you.

Before presenting these exercises, however, let me digress just a little to make an important general explanation:

Throughout this book, at various points, you will find a number of creative-problem-solving exercises. Strictly speaking, not all of them are of "true" creative (many-possible-answer) type. Some are of analytical (few- or single-answer) type. Whatever the type, however, they have been carefully selected for, and are intended to accomplish, these purposes:

1. Provide illustration of key points made in the main text of this book.
2. Stimulate your imagination.
3. Provide you with means of gaining insight into your own, habitual mental processes—to improve them.
4. Provide you with effective practice toward the development of skill in the application of the principles, tools and techniques of Creative Thinking.

You may skip these exercises, or laze through them, or "fudge on" them, if that is your wish. But I am obliged to tell you that in so doing you will cheat yourself.

If you are really serious about improving your creative ability, please, *please* carry out each and every one of these exercises—and do so exactly in accordance with the directions given.

Back on track, now . . .

To carry out these exercises, you will need a pencil, some scratch paper, and a watch (with a second hand). As soon as you have obtained these, proceed.

Exercise 1. Allow yourself *exactly one minute* to complete this assignment: Create new ideas—as many as you can, on any subject—and jot them down. *Start right now.*

Now, pause for a moment. Don't continue thinking about the exercise just finished, because it is just that—finished. Get ready for the next one. Here's how:

1. Get another sheet of paper.
2. Think about your automobile. Does it have some feature

—such as "blind" rearward visibility, for example—that particularly bothers you, irritates you, or dissatisfies you?

3. Jot down a brief, identifying note about the car-fault you have selected. Put it at the top of your sheet of paper, and look at it for a few moments.

4. Now, go on to Exercise #2.

Exercise 2. Allow yourself *exactly one minute* to complete this assignment: Create new ideas—as many as you can—for correcting the automobile-fault that you noted a moment ago— and jot down your ideas. *Start right now.*

Now check the results obtained in the two exercises. For the moment, disregard the quality of the ideas produced. Check only the quantity of new ideas, Exercise #1 *vs.* Exercise #2.

In presenting these exercises to hundreds of different people, over a period of years, I have found that hardly anyone gets a single honest-to-goodness new idea during the first exercise, but that most people are able to generate between two and five genuinely new ideas (new to *them,* remember) during the second exercise. How do you account for this? Did you get a similar result? Why?

These two exercises were designed to serve two purposes. (We'll get to the second purpose later. For now . . .) The first purpose was to take some of the mystery and hot air out of the subject, and show you—via direct, immediate, personal experience—that *you already have CT ability!* It is not something entirely new that you must acquire; i.e., "from scratch." You already have it.

The fact is, as evidenced by the results of tests much greater in scope and depth than our two little exercises, that *every* person has some capacity for CT. So the question is not, "How do we get it?" at all. For we've got it.

But here is "the rub": Psychological studies have indicated repeatedly that the average person regularly uses *less than 50%* of the capacity he already has. The great American philosopher-psychologist, William James, near the end of a lifetime of study, concluded that average usage is about 25%. And some authorities even say, ". . . less than *10%!*"

So the first big question is this:

How can we put more of our present CT capacity to use?

Third

WHAT IS IT—REALLY?

How can we put to use more of the CT capacity which we already have? How can we raise the efficiency of our idea-generating machinery above the indicated present level of ten to fifty per cent?

Before we attempt to answer these questions, perhaps we had better approach the even-more-basic one: *What IS thinking? How does it work? What makes it operate? What is its essential nature? What kind of systems are involved—mechanical ones, or electrical, or hydraulic, or chemical, or what?*

Since thinking takes place in the brain, perhaps we should study it and find out how it works. This seems to be a sensible approach, so let's take a look . . .

Science has discovered some very remarkable things about the human brain and nervous system. For instance:

The right side of the brain controls the movements of the left side of the body, and vice versa. (Isn't that odd? You'd think it would be just the other way around.)

The nervous system works very much like a wet-cell battery. It generates a DC current of about 1/10 volt, or roughly about one-twentieth as much as a flashlight battery. This electric charge is created by two body chemicals (sodium and potassium) operating on nerve tissues bathed in a fluid which is made up chiefly of water.

Our "electric wires" are made up of nerve fibers. The fibers are comprised of tiny sections. As each section of nerve fiber receives an electrical impulse, it "triggers" a reaction in the next section, and so on, *et cetera.*

Nerve impulses travel at a speed of several hundred miles per hour.

The units that control and direct nerve impulses to some purpose, at various points in our personal circuitry, are tiny devices which function like radio tubes—or, as the British call them, somewhat more descriptively, "electric valves." The capacity of the brain is determined by (among certain other things) the number of these valves. It is interesting to note that the most modern man-made "mechanical (electronic) brain," which is patterned after the human brain, owes its amazing "thinking" capacity to the 25,000 or so electric valves it contains. Since such a machine far outdoes an average human in operations as, for example, high-speed, complex mathematical computation, one might suppose that this is due to its having so many more valves. But not so—the human system has between ten and fifteen *billion* electric valves! So, in truth, the human brain has astronomically greater thinking capacity than any machine man has devised—or possibly ever will devise. (Please note that I said *capacity*. Utilization is something else again.)

> An electronic brain equal in capacity to the human brain, according to the General Electric Company, would require something on this order: (1) a structure larger than the Empire State Building, (2) more electric power than is generated at Niagara Falls, and (3) all of the water flowing over Niagara Falls to cool the machine. Such a machine would further require an army of specialists to "feed" it, care for it, direct it, and interpret its work!
>
> How casually you and I regard this miraculous, portable, self-contained, efficient, powerful, personal, exclusive and private thinking machine that has been *given* to us—tax free. And how little real use we must be making of it!

There is evidence that thinking (of some sort) occurs in parts of the body other than the brain.

By the way . . . Are you by any chance beginning to get the vague feeling that this isn't getting us anywhere? Me, too. So let's step things up a bit.

These scientific findings are all very interesting. But, really, they still don't tell us very much, do they?

What in blue blazes *is* thinking, anyway?!?

I started looking for an answer to this question about 25 years ago (when I thought I knew what thinking is, but didn't, and paid almost disastrously for this complacent assumption). And finally, years later—after studying frustrating reams of complex, abstruse writings on the subject, and asking anybody and everybody who might know—I found *the* one, brief, inclusive explanation. Here it is:

"Thinking is activating catenated psychosynapsis."

So there. Now we know.* Or do we? Let's break it down and see.

The word *activating* isn't too difficult to understand. It means: "energizing," or "making active." *Catenated* means: "connected in a series of links, as a chain." And *psychosynapsis* means: "affording communication between *neurons* in the mind." (Neurons, I am told, are the electric-valve-like devices that were mentioned a few paragraphs back.) Putting all these words together, they seem to mean, "Energizing connected mental communication," or "Moving messages around in the head."

Very helpful, no? *No!*

> This is probably as good a place as any to introduce another odd word that is somewhat relevant, since it refers to a special kind of thinking. This word is—*omphaloskepsis*. The coinage, reportedly, of a British army officer who spent some time in the Orient, omphaloskepsis means "deep thought while contemplating the belly button."
>
> I don't know just what use you might make of this word. Possibly, as a suggestion: If some day your boss should catch you with your feet on the desk, taking an unauthorized forty winks, you might recall the word and have the presence of mind to say to him, "Oh, no, sir—I wasn't sleeping on the job. I was engaged in struggling with company problems through omphaloskepsis."

This sort of explanation is comparable to the one that goes, "You can see through glass because it is transparent"—which sounds pretty good until one discovers that the word *transparent*

---

* Honest Injun—this is the best brief explanation I have been able to find to date. If you know a better one, I'll be most grateful to have it.

is made up from two Latin words meaning "see through"; and hence, the "explanation" actually says: "You can see through glass because it is see-through-able."

Such explanations are about as helpful as Herb Shriner's classic "scientific" one as to why some people never have children —*"Their parents never had any."*

After so much of this kind of investigation/explanation, one finally comes to the realization that science has not yet learned enough about the workings of the human mind to be of much real help in answering the question, "What is thinking?" We have a great deal of scientific information which is highly uninformative.

Until very recent years, science had made even less of an investigation into the special nature of *creative* thinking. In his presidential address to the American Psychological Association in 1950, for instance, Dr. J. P. Guilford pointed out that in the preceding 23 years only about *15/100 of one per cent* of all psychological research could be "classified as definitely bearing on the subject of creativity."

It is apparent, therefore—at the moment—that CT is not in the realm of science at all. Rather, it is primarily an *art*. So we are concerned here with *A*CT: the Art of Creative Thinking.

Fortunately, however, while it may be true that CT is principally an art (at least, for the present), science *has* been making a more intensive study of the subject in the years since 1950. And, as a result of this study, science has made at least three important accomplishments:

Learned many of the cause-and-effect influences that are important to CT.

Discovered significant clues as to some of the fundamental laws involved in the processes of CT. And, as a consequence . . .

Formulated a number of genuinely useful hypotheses, guides and workable theories of CT.

Now, at last, we seem to be getting somewhere!

Little may be known about what thinking actually is—especially Creative Thinking. But something very useful indeed is known about how it works and how to work it.

Fourth

WHAT'S HOLDING US BACK?

W here does all this leave us?

Thus far, it seems, three principal conclusions stand out:

CT is primarily an art—albeit an art strengthened by recent scientific study.
Every one of us has some CT ability.
We regularly use only a fraction of our capacity, of our CT potential.

These conclusions, then, if we accept their validity, seem to make it self-evident that the first appropriate move toward increasing our creativity is not a plunge into a study of methods, procedures or techniques of creative thinking. Rather, we should first try to determine: *What's keeping us from using more, or all, of the CT potential we have now?* What *inhibitors* of CT are hindering us?

If we can discover what these inhibiting hindrances are, and find ways to alleviate them, offset them, or eliminate them, it follows that this, in and of itself alone, will inevitably enable us to increase our creativity—possibly to heretofore-undreamed-of levels.

And here's where the aforementioned recent scientific study begins to help:

Investigation, experimentation and research show that there are *at least a dozen* powerful deterrents to CT—at least a dozen forces that work against the liberation and wider application of our latent creative powers.

In a moment, we'll look into them. But in general recommen-

11

dation, before you examine these so-called CT inhibitors, I suggest that you . . .

Do not merely scan or skim-through the explanation of each of these factors. Rather, read it carefully, and pause from time to time to reflect upon what you have read. (After all, you're reading about *you*.)

Do some introspective analyzing as you read. Try to determine in what way and to what extent each inhibitor affects you and your performance.

Make note, as you go along, of any ideas that occur to you concerning ways to overcome the inhibitors.

Now, one by one, let's examine these twelve *Inhibitors of Creative Thinking* . . .

I. POOR HEALTH

The first inhibitor of CT, and a most powerful one, is—*poor health*.

Science long ago rejected the myth of the Cheshire Cat (the creature with a head but no body) and the Headless Horseman (the creature with a body but no head). When a person is unwell, precisely that is the case—*the whole person* is unwell. Mind, heart, lungs, liver and a lot of other internal mechanisms are affected.

It is not merely in song and fable that the thigh bone is connected to the head bone. In flesh and blood, the human being is an intricately interconnected organism that may hurt in the toe because of an ingrown scalp hair, or hurt in the head because of a sore toe.

Thus, when a person is bothered by either chronic poor health, resulting in low vitality, or by acute or intermittent ailments (headache, sore tooth, etc.), the effect is not "just a physical one." His *general* efficiency is lowered.

Thus, too, when a person is bothered by worry, tension, emotional conflict, anxiety, etc., these "psychological factors" are part of a *total* effect—and one which frequently becomes so obsessive, distracting and debilitating as to make concentration extremely difficult, if not impossible.

If you doubt that poor health is a powerful inhibitor, try this:

1. Think back to the last time you had a severe headache or bad cold. Was it not true, at that time, that you were hard put just to perform simple, routine work, let alone try to cope with difficult new problems?

2. Perform two, equivalent, mathematical calculations—the first one as you normally would, the second one while someone is pinching you hard—and observe the difference.

Now, let's not fall into a trap in connection with this inhibitor. Saying that poor health inhibits CT is *not* saying that poor health makes CT impossible. Nor is it saying that poor health is necessarily a valid excuse for failing to *try* to increase one's creativity —for, as no doubt you have observed, *most* of the world's work, including CT, is done by people who don't feel particularly well.

The point is this: Health problems are intrapersonal problems that interfere with our ability to concentrate upon the extrapersonal problems of CT, especially over highly demanding, extended periods. And easing the problems of health has the effect of easing the job of Creative Thinking.

> Curious glimmer on the side: When I am just about to catch a cold, my mind seems to be unusually sharp and clear, and the task of idea-generation is comparatively easy. But after I've got the cold—nyah!
>
> Have you ever observed any such effect in yourself? How do you account for it? More important: how can it be *used* to advantage?

II. INADEQUATE MOTIVATION

If you and I were to become partners in a business enterprise, and the business prospered, and we decided to try to accelerate its progress by establishing a "Department of Creativity," the chances are great that we would set up some very stringent hiring qualifications for the post of head of the new department: *superior general intelligence* (genius level, of course?) required; *advanced technical education* (PhD, naturally?) a requisite; *etc., etc., etc.* . . .

And the chances are great that we would be wrong!

It might *seem* "logical" to expect that these special capabilities (plus graduation from the "right" schools, with certain grades, keys, *et al?*) are significantly related to success in creativity. But impartial observation and study show that such factors, while perhaps "nice"—and maybe even useful, at times, as for "window dressing"—may be far, far outweighed by the simpler factor: *desire* to create.

History abounds with cases of creative successes by people with seemingly spectacular *lack* of "proper qualification," or even natural endowment, for such successes—but imbued with a tremendous, constant *wanting* to create. Sir Frank Whittle, for example, had demonstrated no brilliant bent for, nor preparation for, innovation—before he conceived his jet engine. The Biro brothers (one a chemist, the other a sculptor, journalist and painter) had no "engineering background" from which welled up their invention, the ball-point pen. Edwin Land was only a twenty-year-old student when he invented the first practical, synthetic light polarizer. (Though possible, is it necessary to go on and on here with cases in point?) But all of these men demonstrated uncommon *determination* to innovate—and with what results!

Now, if strong motivation is so powerful a force *for* creativity, it would seem to follow that an *in*sufficiency of this desire would be a deterrent to CT. And so it is.

An inadequately motivated person makes no effort to undertake CT because he feels no impulsion to do so. He has no real interest in doing anything new and different. Frequently he seems to have no incentive to try to do anything new and different—or, at least, he *feels* that no incentive exists. Manifestly, he is a guy who just doesn't *care*.

In the fundamental if unfortunate analysis, inadequate motivation is one of the most common and detrimental inhibitors of CT.

And what is all this to *you?* Only you can determine that, really, of course. Personally, I doubt that the term, "inadequate motivation," characterizes you, else you wouldn't be reading this book. But it may apply, sometime, to someone about whom you care—as a supervisor, as a parent, or in some other relationship. And, in this latter situation, you may find it advisable to . . .

Be willing to accept the conclusion that some people likely can not, and probably should not, be pushed into undertaking much creative work. CT feels too unnatural to them, too unsuited to them; and compulsion to attempt it in such cases brings about undesirable consequences. There is plenty of other important work in the world that such people can and will do better.

Find the *causes* of the person's apparent disinterest before deciding upon any action whatever. (You may find clues to possible causes in this very section of this book.)

Satisfy yourself that no damage will likely result from your application of external motivating pressure. Once so satisfied, go ahead—with understanding.

III. MENTAL LAZINESS

There is good reason to believe that the CT-inhibitor that manifests itself as "inadequate motivation" is closely related, many times, to what is frequently referred to as *mental laziness*.

Frankly, I dislike the term, "mental laziness," for I invariably experience a secret, queasy feeling of guilt upon meeting it. (You too?) I use the term here because it is familiar and easily remembered. But I don't mind telling you that, if I could "have my druthers," I'druther regard the general characteristic to which it alludes in the much kindlier (and perceptive?) way expressed by one of my old teachers:

"Truly," said he, "it is not quite realistic to apply the term, 'mental laziness,' with all of its derogatory implications. Instead, the trait should be described in some such way as, 'A characteristic tendency to conserve energy.' For the fact is that nature has provided us with certain non-volitional defense mechanisms which come into action *automatically* to prevent us from using up our energies beyond the level of reserve which represents some minimum amount needed for our personal safety; that is, to keep us from unwittingly exhausting ourselves to the point of imminent self-harm."

> Forgive me for teasing, but . . . Wasn't that nice of the Prof? Now we can be comfortable with ourselves, knowing that while *other* people may be lazy, which is reprehensible, we higher-type persons simply have "a completely natural tendency to conserve energy"—which is respectable.

However we describe or define this inhibitor, though, the hard,

cold truth remains that the cold, hard *work* of CT upsets, repels
and even overwhelms many people. There's no use trying to
"duck" it—CT *does* imperatively require new effort, new adjust-
ments, new work. And to avoid this work, the mentally lazy
generally resort to one, several or all of four artful dodges:

1. *Rationalization.* "It can't be done," they'll say. Or, "Unrealistic." And so on and so forth. And if they keep repeating
this loud enough and long enough, presently they will have
convinced both themselves and most of those around them—
and, sure enough, "it" effectively *can't* be done—so, as any
darn' fool can plainly see, there's no use wasting any effort
on it!

2. *Disparagement.* "Pipe dreams!" they'll sneer. And if
they recruit at mere arm's length, plenty of others will be found
there to confirm and lend conviction to this denouncement.
So it becomes "obvious" to all the world that nothing should
be done—whereupon, indeed, nothing *will* be done—and anyone who dares to venture that "Mebbe it could . . ." is clearly
an idiot, day-dreamer, idler and wastrel!

3. *Evasion.* "We're much too busy with other things—
important things," they'll say. And undoubtedly they *are* busy,
albeit not half as busy as they will become, five seconds after
it is suggested that they spend some time thinking up new
ideas. And, goodness knows, there is always *something* urgent
waiting for busy people to do as soon as the current tasks are
caught up with. So, "self-evidently," it is impossible to find
any "free time" to fritter away in building air castles!

4. *Intentional Stupidity.* (Believe it or not!) "Gee, we're
sorry . . . we just don't get it—it's 'way over our heads," they'll
say. And this, of course, plants the kiss of death on any hopes
for CT from them; for how on earth could anyone in his right
mind expect creative thinking (whatever that is) from people
who freely admit that they can't think?

To our eternal loss, every one of these human dodges is a
virtually unassailable ("logical, practical, reasonable") explanation as to why the mentally lazy "must" conserve their energies
by not thinking.

There's a very old saying that goes like this: "Five per cent of the people think; five per cent think they think; five per cent will think if they have to; and the rest would rather *die* than think." Now, this saying may or may not be true. (Certainly it is an extremely harsh conclusion!) But if it is true, perhaps it becomes a little less shocking when we consider it in the light of the *demands* of CT. For instance:

Science has estimated that, even when asleep, the human brain consumes about 25 per cent of our available nervous energy. Ophthalmologists have found indications that normal *seeing* uses about 25 per cent. And it is estimated that intensive concentration may consume 75 per cent or more.

Dr. Preston K. Munter, of M.I.T. and Harvard University, in telling the participants in a 1956 "Seminar on Creative Engineering" about some of the findings of research, reported that "A man trying to figure out an engineering problem burns as much sugar—as many calories—as the fellow who breaks the four-minute mile."

One group of researchers, measuring the blood-sugar content (the "fuel supply") of a group of executives engaged regularly in hard mental work, found what they called *executive syndrome*. That is, these executives, sitting at desks and "beating their brains out" over problems, began to get low blood sugar around eleven o'clock in the morning, whereupon they were "all poohed out." They were first thought to be, or to have been, diabetic. But this proved to be untrue. Instead, it was found: When we think—especially against the resistance of difficult problems—we are burning blood sugar at a high rate. Sometimes we use up all the sugar we have, and then we are exhausted.

Small wonder that we are "lazy"—that we have "a characteristic tendency to conserve energy"! Creative Thinking truly *is* unusually exhausting work, leaving precious little energy for other activities.

If this were the end of the matter, there is little doubt but that it would be just that: the end of all attempts at CT—by any of us. Fortunately, however, scientific research has also revealed the other side of the coin:

The human brain is very much like a muscle in the respect

that (1) *it is quickly refreshed and restored by food and rest,* and (2) *it grows steadily stronger with exercise.*

All of which seems to bring us full circle to the very point from which we started: *Our own mental laziness keeps us from being as creative as we are basically capable of being.*

IV. LACK OF CURIOSITY

Did you ever observe a group of people at a time when someone showed the group some strange object or device? If so, you probably also observed that some person in the group glanced idly at the object, seemed to say to himself, "Yup, there it is, all right," then returned to whatever he had been doing before. Some other fellow in the group probably reacted quite differently, though: he was intrigued by the object—he could hardly wait to get his hands on it, to examine it closely, to ask questions about it.

The first person, the non-curious one, learned nothing from the experience. It is doubtful that, ten minutes afterward, he could even recall having *had* any particular "experience."

But the second person, the curious one, not only learned something new—he undoubtedly found his imagination stimulated by the experience. And that is the very kind of stimulation that leads most surely to *new,* creative thinking.

Curiosity is reputed to have killed a cat, once upon a time. Maybe it truly did . . . and maybe this is just another lazy rationalization, too. But, whether it did or didn't, *we* are not brainless cats. We know that intelligent curiosity makes for a *safer* and *better* world for us "cool cats." We know, too, that curiosity—generally in organized form—has led our world to greater progress in the past 50 years than was made in the previous 500.

> All right, I will agree: we have made tragically little progress in human relations during the past 2,000 years. Does this disprove the point, though; or, rather, does it simply point up the truth that we have invested shamefully little of our creative ability in the task of solving the problems of human relations?

While we're in the business of re-examining old sayings, by

the way, perhaps we had better look at the relevant maxim, "Necessity is the mother of invention." The look is revealing . . .

"It ain't necessarily so," say most innovators. There was no great public clamor, for instance, for the airplane, the automobile, the electric light and a lot of other things at the time they were being invented. On the contrary, the inventors just wondered if they could make these things work, figured they could, went ahead and made them work—then waited years for people to *accept* them as "necessities."

> Holy smokes! note: Leading public figures repeatedly told the Wright Brothers that their invention was neither needed nor wanted, and they had been flying a plane for two years when the patent office informed them that the thing was impossible.

In the considered analysis of most thoughtful students of Creative Thinking, progress derives from three things which might be considered attitudinal states:

1. *Dissatisfaction*. The potential innovator dislikes some condition or thing as he finds it. It irritates him, bothers him, somewhat as a bit of foreign matter irritates an oyster into starting a pearl.

2. *Curiosity*. The dissatisfied, potential innovator wonders, "*Why* is it as it is? Suppose . . . Does it have to be? What if . . .? I wonder what would happen . . .?" And what else is this but CT?

3. *Desire for Change*. The dissatisfied, curious, potential innovator is no mere, griping noseybody. He is a man determined to *do* something positive and constructive about changing-for-the-better the unsatisfactory thing which has aroused him to wonder.

No, it takes more than necessity to mother invention. And one of the things it takes a great deal of is—*curiosity*.

V. SUPERFICIALITY

A distressingly common (and unnecessary?) inhibitor of CT is *superficiality*. This means thinking which, according to the dictionary, is "Concerned only with the obvious or apparent . . .

Not profound; not thorough; not given to soundness . . . Shallow; hasty; lacking in depth or substantial qualities . . . Not penetrating beneath the surface, nor farther than the easily or quickly apprehended features of a thing . . ."

The superficial mind works something like this: "Two plus two is four; two times two is four; therefore, any number added to itself will produce a sum equal to the product of that number multiplied by itself." Investigation of just one more example would, of course, reveal the fallacy of this conclusion—but the superficial mind is "concerned only with the apparent . . ."

The creative mind is not content to settle for the obvious. Young "Charlie" Kettering, for instance, *could* have settled for the (proven!) engineering formulas showing that electrical starting of an automobile would require batteries and an electric motor larger than the car-engine itself—in which case we might still be hand-cranking our cars today. But, instead, he looked beyond the obvious and found that the formulas didn't apply in this instance, for they pertained only to equipment to be operated for hours at a time, whereas an auto-engine starter would be called upon for only short "spasms" of power.

Profundity, *per se,* may not necessarily be synonymous with creativity. But superficiality surely *is* one of the greatest, single causes of faulty, *non*-creative thinking. The superficial mind invests mere minutes in matters that may actually require years of thought—and then and thereby consistently produces not worthwhile new ideas, but "flops", "crackpottery" and "duds."

Unhappily, this tendency to produce ideas-too-soon-arrived-at is more prevalent than many realize. The files of our patent office and most industrial suggestion systems, for example, show that fully 75 *per cent* of all the ideas submitted to them are unworkable *because they are superficial*—in both original conception and development.

VI. REPRESSIVE TRAINING AND EDUCATION

At a very early age, strongly repressive influences are brought to bear upon many youngsters.

How recently, in some home you know, for example, have you heard, "Junior, get that junk cleaned up this very minute!"

—when Junior was tinkering, experimenting, exploring, using his natural curiosity to learn, applying his imagination, trying to think creatively? Or, "Children should be seen and not heard"—when the children were noisily trying to think up new games, new words, new songs, new something, new *ideas?*

> No, I do *not* advocate complete license. Understanding, yes.
> Freedom to develop, yes. Encouragement to use imagination, yes.

The result of such repression, if continued to any great degree of intensity and for any appreciable period of time, is that the youngsters become quite well trained indeed—in conformity. And if by chance, as grown-ups, they discover how they have been shackled, and then decide to try to break free into greater creativity, they find they must undergo long, arduous, costly re-training to regain what they had originally as youngsters—until it was trained *out* of them.

Our *educational* practices frequently repress creativity, too. In many of our schools, colleges and universities, the emphasis is all too commonly upon . . .

> • *Learning by rote*—conforming to fixed programs of in-formation-stuffing; gathering of information without corre-sponding *understanding* of that information. The famed educator, Dr. Nathaniel Cantor, attests that "The essential goal of the American college remains that of fact-gathering." Yet, as educators well know, about 90% of all rote learning is forgotten within 24 hours after it has been "learned."
>
> • *Pursuing rigid curricula*—completing hoary, prescribed, past-centered courses only because, too frequently, "It's re-quired. Tradition . . . That's the way it's done at dear, old Podunque U."
>
> • *Learning outmoded disciplines*—learning ancient meth-ods and knowledges which have to be abandoned immediately upon graduation because they are completely out of harmony with the more modern practices and findings that have super-seded them in "the outside world." (Pet peeve in point: Eng-lish as taught vs. English as used.)
>
> • *Rewarding the merely tractable,* to the penalty of the genuinely imaginative—bestowing "A's" upon the docile little

souls who write neatly, do all their homework, keep their noses clean, never argue (and promptly forget everything "learned" as soon as the grades are issued), while assigning mere passing grades and "trouble-maker" labels to the intellectually vigorous students who question the book, are skeptical of stock answers, or otherwise upset the placidity of classrooms by showing interest in subjects that goes beyond the books. (Isn't it palpably plain, by the way, that the very finest and latest of books is—and can only be—a record of what *has been* learned or opined, not what is yet to be discovered?)

There are at least five reasons why such educational practices inhibit CT:

1. They stop *short* of CT. They impart information without teaching how to apply it to the creation of *new* ideas.

2. They compel students to restrain their natural desire to create until they have "mastered present course content"— by which time they are usually firmly entrenched in the *habit* of refraining from CT.

3. They encourage *imitation*—to the discouragement of creation. (Teachers of the arts may be the most obvious offenders in this respect. For instance, no less an authority than Arturo Toscanini once said that the only real creativity evidenced in music in the twentieth century was in the field of —of all things!—American *jazz*. And other authorities have said that if Brahms, Chopin and others were alive today, they would undoubtedly be leading composers of jazz. Ask the average music teacher about jazz, however, and you will find that it is a dirty word.)

4. They tempt the student too often to settle for the quickest, simplest, first-that-will-work, easiest-to-arrive-at answers that will get passing grades—and, frequently, also to assume complacently that these are "the", final, or complete, ultimate, or best answers, when in reality the most that can be said for them is that they are merely the easiest-to-obtain answers of the moment in a world wherein answers of all sorts are forever being rendered obsolescent by newer discoveries.

5. They implant the notion that the end-purpose of educa-

tion is the mere accumulation/memorization of (dubious) facts, when in all reality the proper end-purpose of education is no such static thing—it is dynamic: it is to bring about *intelligent action,* which is practically synonymous with *creation.*

But practices of this kind are not exclusive to schools, colleges or universities. Industry, for instance, is not much different. From the moment many a new employee is hired, it is impressed upon him that "Here's the way we do things around here. Now, don't start getting any ideas for changes. Do it the way we tell you, because we've had experience in this business." And no doubt this is all right and proper—up to a point. The trouble is that it usually gets *over*-done to the point where the employee becomes thoroughly imbued with the belief that the only way he can get approval—and avoid suspicion, disapproval, rejection, even the loss of his job—is to conform, to be like all the others around him (who have previously been similarly "trained"). And this is just exactly the antithesis of the spirit of Creative Thinking.

When we look penetratingly into the whole pattern of our training and educational practices, it becomes painfully evident that some of them are devilishly well designed to inhibit, even prevent, CT. Many of our leading educational institutions and industries recognize this, of course; and many have wisely initiated full-fledged CT courses at the adult level. It is deeply to be hoped that similar wisdom may soon lead to provision of general creativity-training for younger students before they develop the educated constriction of the imagination that has so hampered their elders.

VII. JOB DEGRADATION

The literature of business, industry and government today is full of talk about the need for "generalists," scientists, administrators, technicians, thinkers, engineers—more capable, creative people in general.

Yet, in every sizable organization, it is easy to find uniquely capable men and women burdened with tasks that could be performed just as well or better by persons of lesser ability and training. We are short of "talent"—yet we continue to use such people in work that neither permits use of, nor challenges, their special mental abilities. Thus we accomplish a doubly detrimental result: (1) we prevent the unusually qualified from making the greatest use of what they've got; and (2) we prevent the less-well-qualified from progressing to the work they need for their own satisfaction, best utilization and further development.

We may be even more wasteful of high-potential creative talent in another area: With our planned fractionation and simplification of industrial jobs, over the years, we have so starved many of them that they now require little more than robot reaction. We have so stripped these jobs of interest and dignity as to make it almost inevitable for the people performing them either to atrophy mentally or be forced to find outlets for their mental energies in such destructive activities as agitation, horseplay, or making games out of seeing how much can be "put over on the company."

But perhaps the most tragic example of waste of latent creativity is to be found in the case of *the man who degrades his own job*—the man who spends so much time on what is "urgent" that he never has time or energy left for what is *important*—the man who is forever occupied and preoccupied with the trivial, routine, inconsequential or insignificant. It is axiomatic that "A poor porter sweeps better than the best president." But how very many "presidents" we see, doing the porters' jobs!

C. F. Kettering once said, "The opportunities in this world are as great as we have imagination to see them; but we never get the view from the bottom of a rut." Yet a rut is precisely what many of us dig for ourselves by steadfastly refusing to upgrade ourselves in our jobs.

VIII. _____
(Fill in the name of this inhibitor later.)

As you see, the name of Inhibitor VIII has been omitted, above. You'll find the same thing for later ones, too. And there is reason for this. I am trying to: (1) prevent you from working against yourself by bringing detrimental preconceptions into play; (2) provide you an opportunity for constructive activity, as opposed to passivity; (3) make this whole experience more interesting for you; and (4) provide you with vivid, significant experience from which you can draw personally useful understanding.

Is your curiosity aroused? Good. Let's satisfy it. Get pencil and paper, and follow the directions below.

Allow yourself *exactly one minute* to solve this problem in *Nuclear Physics:* (Start *now.*)

Yesterday you computed erg velocity. You therbled five nucleonics, as shown below. Compute the sum of these in fissioncybers.

		Fissioncybers
1	mass-velocity erg unit @ 14 blig points	.69
1	multiple coordinate @ .031254 inertial value	.12
3	millitherbs @ force-velocity E:mc2 plus/minus	1.78
1	full-entity hydronucleus @ 3.2 square of unit	.32
2	electronuclear hygrocarbols @ force .89 pH2 std.	.97
	Total fissioncybers	___

Now increase these f/c's by 3% to find ultimate erg velocity.
    Now go right on to the next problem.

Allow yourself *exactly one minute* to solve this problem in *Industrial Engineering:* (Start *now.*)

Yesterday you made a time-and-motion study. You timed five elements, as shown below. Find the total time for these elements in decimal minutes.

	Decimal Minutes
Pick up assembly and place in position	.32
Run cutting tool 3.750″ to starting position	.12
Make three cuts, .025″ each, 2.500″ apart	1.78
Re-position assembly and set gauge at "0" point	.97
Inspect assembly and put aside in #89 bin	.69
Total decimal minutes	___

Now increase this time by 3% to find the standard allowance.
    Proceed at once to the next exercise.

Allow yourself *exactly one minute* to solve this problem in *Shopping:* (Start *now.*)

Yesterday you went shopping. You bought five items, as shown below. Find the total cost of these items.

		Money spent
1 box of carpet tacks @ 12¢ per box		$ .12
1 tube of toothpaste @ 32¢ per tube		.32
3 cans of scouring powder @ 23¢ per can		.69
1 car-polishing kit @ 97¢ per kit		.97
2 cans of floor wax @ 89¢ per can		1.78
	Total money $	

Now add a 3% sales tax to find out what you spent altogether.

Now, check the answers you obtained in the three exercises—and let's see . . .

The problem is really *the same one* in each of the three exercises. That is, essentially each one amounts to this: Add five decimal numbers (which come to 3.88), increase the total by 3% (which is .1164), and obtain the answer—3.9964. Is this the way you handled it? If not, why not?

In presenting these three exercises to hundreds of different people (usually in somewhat controlled groups) I have found this: Practically everyone readily solves the "Shopping" problem, for it is a familiar type and causes no particular difficulty. Those who *try* (and about half of them will) are usually successful in solving the so-called "Industrial Engineering" problem—if they refuse to be dismayed by their "lack of background in the subject." And a great many people are so overwhelmed by the over-my-headness of the fake "Nuclear Physics" problem that their brains congeal, and all thinking ceases.

There are no doubt several factors involved in the explanation as to why our thinking is somewhat faulty (shaky?) when dealing with problems such as those in these exercises. One of the factors—indeed, I believe, by far the most important one—is that powerful inhibitor of CT . . .

EMOTION-MINDEDNESS

The *feelings* we have about things tend to distort them and to interfere with our ability to think clearly, objectively and creatively about them.

In a 1954 survey by a leading opinion-research organization, for example, a group of union members who were asked about the so-called Taft-Hartley Law were strongly "against it." But when they were asked about each specific, key provision (*e.g.,* prohibition of Communist union leaders) of "another law"— which was actually the same Taft-Hartley, unidentified—they were even more strongly *"in favor"*!

Some authorities estimate that the average person is about 80 per cent emotional and 20 per cent logical.

> You and I, of course, are exceptions—we are completely objective, rational and logical. And for proof of this, I offer:
> 1. Each of us spends "only a few hundred" dollars of his annual income for alcohol, cosmetics, outboard motors, neckties, tobacco, etc.—because these things are absolutely necessary to the maintenance of life on the planet Earth.
> 2. Each of us has or is determined to get a $4,000, 300 h.p., 4,000-pound, 100 m.p.h., power-assisted mobile boudoir —which is the most efficient device available for traveling 25 m.p.h. (without getting wet) to the corner drugstore to buy the abovementioned necessities of life. And . . .
> 3. Each of us men has contracted for the total, lifetime support of some girl who isn't even related to us—for the logical reason that this is the best and most economical way to obtain regular meals and clean laundry.
>
> Forgive me for teasing . . . but we *are* trying to be honest with ourselves, and find out what's keeping us from being more creative, aren't we?

Probably our greatest emotional problem relative to CT is— *fear* . . .

> Fear of the risk involved in pioneering.
> Fear of making mistakes and appearing foolish.
> Fear of losing the psychological safety of the known, the familiar.
> Fear of expending time/money/energy with no assurance of success.
> Fear of being "different"—when society exerts such constant pressure on us to "conform to the norm."
> And so on.

We have other emotional problems, too, such as . . .

> Over-anxiety for quick success.

Over-dependence upon past experience.
Unwillingness to give up or alter biased opinions.
And so on.

And they all add up to this:

Our emotion-mindedness keeps us from being as creative as we are fundamentally capable of being.

IX. _____
(Fill in the name of this inhibitor later.)

If you carried out the foregoing three-exercise project according to directions, you probably got a "kick" out of it—and learned something important about *yourself*, as well. So, let's follow the same general plan again, and see if we can obtain a similar value.

Interested? Fine! Get paper and pencil, follow the directions, and carry out these exercises:

1. Allow yourself *five minutes* to rearrange the letters O-W-D-E-N-A-R-W to spell a new word—but not a proper name, nor anything foreign or "unnatural". Write it out.
2. Quickly, now: How many animals of each species did Adam take aboard the Ark with him? (Note that the question is not how many *pairs,* but how many *animals.*)
3. What unusual characteristic do these six words have in common?:
    DEFT   SIGHING   CALMNESS   CANOPY   FIRST   STUN
    (Please complete your answer within five minutes.)
4. Figure out this problem in diplomatic relations: If an international airliner crashed *exactly* on the U.S.-Canadian border, where would they be required by international law to *bury* the survivors? (If you can't decide within one minute, please go on to the next item.)
5. What is the minimum number of active baseball players on the playing field during any part of an inning? How many "outs" in each inning?
6. Figure out this problem within *one minute:* If one face of a cube measures 2″ x 4″, what is the area of *each* of

the faces, and what is the *total* area of all eight faces?
(Jot your answer in the margin.)

7. A farmer had 17 sheep. All but nine died. How many did he have left?

8. An archeologist reported finding two gold coins dated 46 B.C. Later, at a dinner in his honor, he was thoroughly and openly discredited by a disgruntled fellow archeologist. Why?

9. A man living in Winston-Salem, North Carolina, may not be buried in a state west of the Mississippi River—nor in Hawaii or Alaska—even in the event of Presidential intervention. Why is this?

10. If you went to bed at 8:00 o'clock last night, and set your alarm clock to get up at 9:00 o'clock this morning, why on earth—after thirteen hours' rest, especially!—are you so sleepy today?

11. If you had only one match, and entered a room to start up a kerosene lamp, an oil heater, and a wood-burning stove, which would you light first—and why?

12. Quickly, now: Divide 30 by ½, and add 10. What is the answer?

13. If your doctor gave you three pills, and told you to take one every half-hour, how long would it require for you to take all of them?

14. Two men played checkers. They played five games, and each man won three. How do you explain this?

15. Look at these phrases, for a moment, to get them firmly in mind:

Now look away, and write down these exact phrases from memory.

*   *   *

Now, if you have completed all 15 of the exercises—and only then, please!—proceed. Check your answers against the following:

Re Exercise 1: The directions told you to "Rearrange the letters O-W-D-E-N-A-R-W to spell a new word . . ." So you should have spelled—A NEW WORD. Did you?

Re Exercise 2: There is nothing in recorded history to indicate that *Adam* took any animals aboard the Ark. The fellow with the Ark was *Noah.* No? Ah!

Re Exercise 3: Each of the six words—*deft, sighing, calmness, canopy, first, stun*—contains three letters of the alphabet in regular alphabetical order. Unusual, isn't it? And is that what you recorded?

Re Exercise 4: Now, really! It would hardly be conducive to good international relations to "bury the *survivors,*" do you think?

Re Exercise 5: Besides the nine players for the fielding team, at least one opponent—a batter—will have to be on the field before there can be an "old ball game." And *each* team is allowed three "outs," for a total of *six* "outs" per inning. Did you mark "10" and "6," then?

Re Exercise 6: I'll bet you noticed right away that this isn't a proper problem at all—because a cube has neither *rectangular* faces nor *eight* faces. This *is* what you noticed, isn't it?

Re Exercise 7: If "all *but* nine" of the farmer's sheep died, nine is the number he had left.

Re Exercise 8: The coins were dated "46 B.C.", hmmm? And "B.C." means *"Before* Christ" . . . 'Nuf sed.

Re Exercise 9: If a man is *"living* in Winston-Salem"—or any other place—his burial *now* would be quite out of order, no? Yes.

Re Exercise 10: If you went to bed at 8:00 o'clock, and set your alarm clock for 9:00 o'clock, the alarm sounded *one hour later.* Those crazy clocks . . . can't tell night from day, y'know!

Re Exercise 11: A fellow planning to light something with a match will likely light the *match* first, no? . . . Sort of necessary, seems like.

Re Exercise 12: 30, divided by ½ (or .5), is 60. And 60 plus 10 is 70. So it's plain as can be that the answer is *not* 25.

Re Exercise 13: If you took the first pill at 3:00 o'clock, the second one in a half-hour, at 3:30, and the third one at the end of another half-hour, i.e., at 4:00 o'clock, the three pills would all have gone "down the hatch" in the span of one hour. Right? Right!

Re Exercise 14: The two fellows playing checkers were plainly not playing checkers with each other, but with two other checker players.

Re Exercise 15: Well, of course, you had no trouble seeing that there were two "the's" in "Paris . . .," two "a's" in "Once . . . ," and so on. Or did you?

*　　*　　*

If you made two correct observations in these fifteen exercises, congratulations! Many people—regardless of intelligence, education, environment, influence, "push", or what have you—don't make *any*.

And just what were these exercises supposed to show? I'm sure you already know: One of the most common and severe inhibitors of CT is . . .

FAULTY OBSERVATION

One psychologist has described this all-too-human characteristic as, "The inability to see the obvious." And after the experience you have just had with the fifteen exercises, it must be quite obvious that this inability-to-see-the-obvious severely handicaps us in our efforts to get the *information* needed for sound, creative thinking.

But as though this were not difficulty enough, it is evident that we also observe *selectively*—we "screen out" or "screen in"; we look for what we *wish* to look for (period.), or for what *interests* us; or, we notice only what we're *accustomed* to noticing (question mark?); or, we see only what we *expect* to see (exclamation point!).

It's a little hard (!) to see this characteristic in oneself (and you've already been through enough exercises in point), but you can spot it readily in others through this little experiment:

Draw this . . .

. . . show it to someone, and ask, "What is it?" The odds are scads-to-one that your observer will quickly respond, *"Four!"* Whereupon you can show that quite conspicuously you had drawn not a "four" at all, but only a few simple lines—and the *observer* had mentally filled-in additional lines to form the numeral "4." And if the observer insists, "What else *could* it be?" you can show that your sketch might be of a part of any number of different objects, such as a paddle wheel . . .

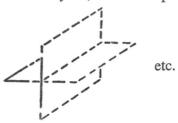

etc.

We *can't* think—creatively, analytically, judiciously, or what-have-you-ly—with knowledge we don't have. We can think only with the information we *do* know. And if we can not observe accurately, we can not obtain accurate information with which to do accurate thinking.

Further: if we do not observe well, *we do not even perceive the existence of problems* that desperately need the attention of creative minds.

The ability to perceive/observe accurately is of critical importance to sound Creative Thinking. Indeed, it is practically *sine qua non*—that without which there is nothing.

X. JUDICIAL-MINDEDNESS

If you were a student in a "live" CT Course, it is doubtful that your instructor would at this point tell you the name of Inhibitor X. It is probable, instead, that he would ask you to take part in some such experiment as the following:

Step 1: Divide the class into three "CT Teams."

Step 2: Send Team #1 out of the room.

Step 3: Tell Team #2 to remain in the room and serve as observer-reporters during the entire experiment.

Step 4: Lead Team #3 through a five-minute CT session wherein they think up all the ideas they can "for improving the dining room table"—and do so *ad lib,* uninhibitedly, and without criticism, evaluation or commentary of any kind. Record all of the ideas (as quick, brief notes on a large easel-pad, chalkboard, etc.) as they are suggested; and, when the time is up, count the total number of ideas generated by the team.

Step 5: Tell Team #3 that Team #1 will be asked to hold an identical kind of session, but that, while they are so doing, Team #3 is to criticize each idea as it is presented—and to do so fairly but firmly.

Step 6: Recall Team #1 to the room, and proceed as in "Step 5," above. Record and count the ideas generated by this team. Then compare the results produced by Team #3 vs. Team #1.

Step 7: Ask Team #2 to report on what they observed— and what it means. Ask Team #1 to explain how they felt under the pressure of criticism. Carry out a general group discussion, and ask the group to summarize its conclusions concerning the experiment and its results.

This experiment invariably points up the conclusion that Creative Thinking and criticism are unnatural bedfellows—that concurrent flaw-spotting is the deadly enemy of creativity—and that people "thinking up" in a permissive, encouraging atmosphere, in a favorable attitudinal climate, generate more and better ideas than when trying to create in a critical atmosphere. Further: this conclusion applies to criticism from *whatever source*—be it outside, or from within the person-trying-to-create, himself.

It is a well-proven principle of psychology that abilities tend to atrophy under fault-finding, but flourish under encouragement. Yet few of us are free from impulses toward hasty, premature, "reflex" criticism. When George Westinghouse took his air brake for trains to that "progressive railroader," Commodore Vanderbilt, for instance, the Commodore threw him out, saying, "I have no time for fools." And when Henry Ford tried to set up his first assembly line, he had to get rid of his first engineers— men who *"knew"* it couldn't be done—and accomplish the job with men who *didn't* know it couldn't be done, so went ahead and did it!

Is your tendency different? Check back and see: what did you *really* think when you first heard of zippers, ball-point pens, instant coffee and/or any other then-new things?

Here again, we can trace at least part of the origin of this tendency to certain educational philosophies and practices. There is one school of thought in education, for example, which holds that: "The prime purpose of education is to equip the student to *discriminate* between good and bad, to determine what is first-rate." The efforts of teachers so grounded and motivated are, therefore, bent toward training their pupils to *judge*—which means training them primarily to analyze and *criticize*, not to create.

Now, the point of all this discussion is that, as shown by recent investigations, "judicial-mindedness" inhibits, impedes, discourages and sometimes completely defeats CT. The point is *not* that judgment should be eliminated, which would be patently ridiculous. The point is that evaluation should occur *at the right time*—which is *after* the new ideas have been formulated, not while CT is in progress.

This point was summarized very aptly in a talk at a leading midwestern university by Alex Osborn, the man who has probably contributed more toward the development of a creative-education movement than anyone else in America. Osborn said, "When ideation (creation) is unhampered by criticism, the average person can produce *ten times* as many ideas—in the same length of time—as when judgment is allowed concurrently to interfere."

XI. ———————
(Fill in the name of this inhibitor later.)

Before getting into any discussion at all of Inhibitor XI, I am going to tell you about a wonderful product and a wonderful opportunity for you to capitalize on its possibilities.

Research, as you know, has in recent years accomplished near-miracles in developing new materials—materials such as synthetic fibers, alloys, chemicals, plastics, ceramics, and so on. And, thanks to a group of enlightened executives, who ask for no credit or publicity for this, I am enabled to inform you here and now about such a material—dubbed, simply, "Material X"—

which not only has some remarkable properties, but (here's your big break:) since it will not be patented, will be available to anyone who can develop uses for it.

Here are some of the qualities of this amazing material:

It is a solid.

It is non-corrosive.

It is a non-conductor of electricity.

It can be made in virtually any color.

It is one of the most inexpensive basic materials ever developed.

It can be made in an almost unlimited variety of shapes and sizes.

It can be produced and processed on existing machinery, in great quantities, from plentiful supplies of raw materials.

It is lighter than metal.

It can be made flexible or inflexible.

It resists the passage of heat and sound.

It can be made to absorb or reflect light.

It can be made either durable or short-lived.

It can be made combustible or non-combustible.

It has good shear strength and impact resistance.

It can be made opaque, translucent or transparent.

It has fair abrasion resistance and flexing qualities.

It can be made with a rough, smooth or textured surface.

It can be made dimensionally stable or dimensionally variable.

It can be made to resist the action of various chemical substances.

It can be made absorbent or adsorbent, or non-absorbent/non-adsorbent.

It can be made to resist penetration by gases, oils, vapors, greases, etc.

It can be made to resist the effects of sunlight, fungus attack, weathering, aging, etc.

Pound for pound, as in laminated-sheet form, for example, it has higher tensile strength than steel.

It is compatible with other materials such as wood, leather, glass, rubber, metal, textiles, paints, dyes, etc.

Some product-application testing has already been done with this Material X. (A few examples: It has been made into rail-road-car wheels with a life-expectancy of several hundred thousand miles. A factory chimney has been made of it. It has been tried as the major structural material in a small church. Watch parts have been made of it, with excellent results. And it seems to hold up unusually well as paving or surfacing material.) But there are undoubtedly countless other possibilities as yet untried. So the question stands: What uses *can* be made of this amazingly versatile material? What uses can *you* think of?

Please, for *your* sake—if you don't follow directions anywhere else in this book, *do so now:*

> Stop reading the main text right now, and don't resume until you have spent *at least an hour* working on the project of thinking up uses for Material X.
> Start your project by re-reading the foregoing list of the material's qualities/characteristics/properties/attributes.
> Make a list of all the ideas you can think of for possible uses for the material.
> When you seem to be running out of ideas—and only then—put your list aside, temporarily, take a short "break" from your CT work, and then resume reading below.

As you continue reading, in this and in subsequent sections of this book, you will undoubtedly continue to get additional ideas for possible uses for this unique material. And I don't doubt that you will also stop once in a while in the middle of things, so to speak, to jot down ideas that seemingly have come out of nowhere. This is not only "permissible" (as though you needed permission!)—it is entirely natural and desirable.

I would go even further: I would say that you *should* deliberately stop from time to time, get out fresh paper and pencil, restudy the list of the qualities of the material, set some minimum time limit (say 15 minutes), and make a game out of seeing whether you can beat your own previous record for the number of new ideas produced per session. And I will promise you: if you will carry out this plan, I will guarantee that—contrary to what you might believe at this moment—you will not only *not* exhaust all the idea-possibilities in the first few such sessions; you will find that your *best* ideas will occur to you only after you have got the first (and generally superficial) ideas out of the way to clear the path for the genuinely unique ones you have it in your power to create. Give it a real trial, and see.

Oh, say—by the way . . . Did I remember to tell you the commonly preferred name for the material called X? No? Well, then, let's remedy this oversight right now: Material X is paper. Yes, *paper!*

Now, before you "blow your top," and start jumping to hasty conclusions, let me explain:

First, except for the contrived name, every important particular that I gave you about the so-called "Material X"—which is paper—is true.

Second, this material does, indeed, have the qualities listed.

Third, as for "product-application testing," let me quote from the authoritative *Paper Trade Journal:* "At one time the Pullman Company used car wheels made of laminated and compressed paper, and one set is known to have lasted for 300,000 miles. A 50-foot factory chimney was built of paper at Breslau, in Prussia. A paper church served worshipers in a Swedish parish for 30 years. (It was made of paper maché soaked in vitriol water mixed with lime that had been treated with curdled milk and the whites of eggs.) A Dresden watchmaker made a paper watch that, it is said, kept perfect time. Paving bricks have been made of paper, and paper horse shoes were once quite common."[1]

Fourth, it is also true that paper "will not be patented"—because it is not patentable in its basic form.

Finally, I have it on the testimony of respected, authoritative researchers in the paper industry that "It is probable that there are thousands upon thousands more practical uses for paper, in its various forms, than any of us have thus far even begun to imagine."

So, you see, you have been working—and should *continue* working—on a completely real and realistic project. Keep on thinking of paper in this fashion: as Material-X-with-certain-qualities. And keep on thinking up uses for it!

"But," you may say, "surely you had something more in mind than 'tricking' me into thinking creatively about some particular material, beneficial though that may prove to be."

Right! I was trying to give you as vivid a relevant, personal

---

[1] From the *Paper Trade Journal,* 49 West 45th Street, New York, N. Y.

experience as possible; first, to show you how Inhibitor XI can be turned around to work *for* you, not against you; second, to show you how it ordinarily *does* tend to work against you. And in this second connection . . .

Do you see what really happened during this experience? When, at the very beginning, you started thinking from the basis of the *qualities* of the so-called Material X, you fell *naturally* into thinking creatively about it. Was this not true? But if you had started from the basis of the material's common *name* or *label,* it's 100-to-one that you would have been frightened off, or uninterested—or, in any event, *unstimulated* to think creatively about it. You would have said, "Paper is old stuff; give me something *new* to think about." Or, "Paper is too familiar; it has been thoroughly explored; why, the experts have already figured out everything . . ." and that would have been that. Is this not true?

While We're at It

By the way, if "the experts have already figured out everything . . ." why is it that electronic television was invented by a 14-year-old boy, Philo Farnsworth, and not by giant General Electric, Westinghouse, RCA, *et al*—who are "expert" as all get-out and have tremendous resources and research facilities to boot? Why was the Polaroid Camera invented by one man, Edwin Land, and not by the oh-so-overwhelmingly expert giants of the photographic industry? And why was the cyclotron invented by Ernest Lawrence; catalytic cracking of petroleum by Eugene Houdry; Cinerama by Fred Waller; the jet engine by Frank Whittle—not by General Motors, General Dynamics, General Foods, or general-anything-else?

And why . . . Oh, well, I'm sure you see the answer: the experts have *not* "already figured out everything"! Here, for instance, are some things which no one, expert or otherwise, has yet figured out:

> What makes it rain?
> What is normalcy?
> What causes laughter?
> Why is the grass green?
> What is optimal health?

Why do people like music?

What is the nature of life?

Why do people behave as they do?

What are the fundamental laws of nature?

Why do civilizations differ from one another?

Where did the universe come from, and where is it going?

What is the secret of the duplication and organization of cells into organs?

Why do people remember things they have seen better than things they have heard?

Why is the human gestation period nine months instead of six, or twelve, or eighteen, or some other period?

What is the size and shape of the universe?

Where do cosmic rays come from?

What holds the nucleus together?

What is the nature of energy?

Why are galaxies spiral?

What is probability?

What is memory?

What is matter?

The Point

And what (finally, now!) is the point of all this? The point is this: We tend to be *label-minded*—to think from the basis of the *names* of things rather than the uncluttered facts about them —and this causes us to limit, narrow-down, or even *stop* thinking.

Inhibitor XI, then, is . . .

LABEL-MINDEDNESS

Unhappily, as though it were not bad enough that our own tendency toward label-mindedness gets in the way, this characteristic in *others* also seriously impedes, and may on occasion completely block, creativity. This effect was explained in a talk made at Ohio State University by the national recognized authority on semantics, Dr. Hans Sperber: "Where the tyranny of the dictator and the jailkeeper ends, there the tyranny of *words* begins. Words can force our thinking and actions into channels not of our own choosing. They can fetter our thoughts. The lowliest American may bring up any idea—but let somebody succeed in tagging it with a *label*-word like 'unrealistic,' 'radical' or 'idealistic,' and its chances of being scrutinized and judged according to its merits will evaporate."

To lay the dust on this eleventh inhibitor of CT, now—there are probably two key points that are most important to keep in mind:

First, to think most clearly and creatively about anything, we should think from the basis of the *facts* about it, not its mere name or label.

Second, to get others favorably inclined toward our good, new ideas, we should try to get associated with them those label-words that connote *good, constructive, practical, useful, profitable.*

XII. ————————————
(Fill in the name of this inhibitor later.)

The last of the dozen inhibitors of Creative Thinking to be discussed in detail *per se* in this book is one that is both unusually common and uncommonly troublesome. To get personal, useful insight into its nature and effects, now, please perform a pertinent experiment—by carrying out these ten exercises:

1. Make four 9's equal 100. (Not 99.99, or almost 100— *exactly* 100.)
2. Explain why they have a 4th of July in *England,* just as we have in the United States, even though . . . Well, you know your history.
3. Following are two views of a simple, solid object . . .

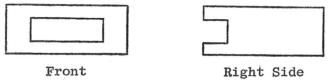

      Front   **Right Side**

Sketch the missing view—the *top* view.
4. A man built a conventional-style, four-sided house, each side having a southern exposure. A big bear wandered past his house one day. What color was the bear?

5. Using six matches of equal length, construct four equilateral triangles, each having the length of a match for one of its sides.

6. As you see, the nine dots in the illustration below can be readily connected with five straight lines . . .

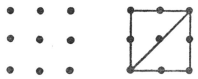

Without lifting your pencil from the paper, once you have started, connect the nine dots with *four* straight lines.

7. A woman gave a beggar 50¢. The woman was the beggar's sister, but the beggar was not the woman's brother. Explain this.

8. Over the work bench in a man's garage there was a square window, the opening of which was 24 inches high and 24 inches wide. This didn't admit enough daylight, however. So the man called in a carpenter, and told him to double the window-opening. Whereupon the carpenter did double it—thereby admitting twice as much light— but whereupon it was *still* a square opening, 24 inches high and 24 inches wide. Explain this.

9. A man may not marry his widow's sister in Ohio. Why is this?

10. Following are two views of a simple, solid object . . .

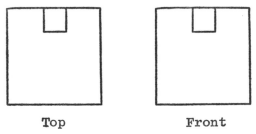

Top   Front

(Yes, the two views are identical.)
Sketch the missing view—the *side* view.

Now, I suppose, you think I'm going to give you the solutions to the ten problems. But I am not. So, if you have found them "tough," and decided that you "don't really need to" solve them to extract full value from this experiment, *quit kidding yourself and get back to work!*

I'll just wait here while you do.

*   *   *

Oh, all right . . . Here are the solutions:

1. 99 9/9 equals 100. And 99/.99 equals 100. No doubt there are other simple solutions, too. Did you get at least one?

2. They have a 4th of July in England—and a 3rd, and 5th, and so on and on—because they use the same kind of calendar as the United States. Now, if you were thinking about the *holiday*, Independence Day . . . but then, that hasn't anything to do with the question, has it?

3. Probably the simplest solution is . . .

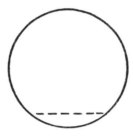

4. If a man built his house at a location where every exposure was a southerly one, he built it at the North Pole. There might, on some occasion, be some other kind of bear there; but, chances are, the one that wandered past his house was a white polar bear.

5. I'll bet you persisted for a long time in trying to solve this one in two dimensions—and got nowhere. So, try *three* dimensions: lay out three of the matches to form an equilateral triangle (on a flat surface), then raise the other three matches from the corners of this triangle to form a pyramid.

6. Why did you insist upon keeping the lines within the square implied by the arrangement of the dots—instead of doing this?:

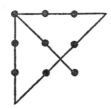

7. Anyone who begs might be called a beggar. A beggar might be male or female. And a *female* beggar might be the sister—but certainly not the brother—of "a woman (who) gave a beggar 50¢." Right? Right!

8. To begin with, the window-opening was like this:

Then the carpenter doubled it, making it like this:

9. Well, now, if a fellow has a widow, he's deceased. And, in this condition, he's not very marriageable—in Ohio or elsewhere.

10. Probably the simplest solution is . . .

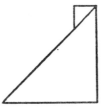

Do you feel a little thick (no lisp intended) about now? Well, if so, welcome to the fraternity, brother! Our members are legion, as they say. Me? I'm a charter member.

Now, what on earth is it that gives us so much trouble in

thinking-through problems such as these? Psychology tells us (and you can go back, now, and fill this in as the name of Inhibitor XII) . . .

CONCEPTUAL BLOCKS

. . . the big idea of which is this:

When we are faced with a problem—*any* problem, be it creative, analytical, judicial, or what-have-you—our first attempt at solving it invariably consists of trying to dredge-up satisfactory solutions (or merely a single solution!) from *old* conceptions, from *past experience,* from *memory.*

If this works, it's wonderful. It's fast, easy, efficient and economical. In fact, we couldn't even get along in life without it! Suppose, for example, that one had to figure out how to tie his shoe strings—*anew*—every time he put on his shoes. Then add this difficulty to all the other "ordinary" problems with which one copes daily, and we can only conclude: *what a remarkable system!*

The trouble with this system, however (or is it with our manner of using it?) is that it frequently becomes so *over*-worked and *totally* relied-upon that it traps us. We depend upon it *exclusively*—and then we become mechanical, inflexible, robot-like, unresourceful, unimaginative.

Is this not what you observed about your own approaches to the ten illustrative problems? In dealing with the tenth one, for instance—the one where, given two (identical) views of an object, you were asked to supply the side view—didn't your memory or past experience tell you that, since the top and front of the object were "square," the object "had to be" a cube? Didn't this conception (all right, *mis*conception) block your path to a correct solution? And didn't this same tendency toward confined conceptualizing hamper you similarly in dealing with the other nine problems, too?

Two types of conceptual blocks seem to be especially prevalent and inhibiting. One is generally called "functional fixation"; the other, "familiarity-focusing." (Together, alliteratively, they might be termed "the 4 F's" of non-CT.)

"Functional fixation" means just about what it seems to mean; that is: we sometimes fix mentally upon a certain function of a thing, and then can not conceive of the thing in connection with any other possible function. An example of this might be found in the confined conception of a carpenter's hammer as *only* a carpenter's hammer—as a pounding, prying or breaking device —not as a possible rocker, heating instrument, anvil, measuring tool, shaping mandrel, etc. *(ad infinitum?)*.

An example of "familiarity-focusing" was once described to me in this commentary by one of America's top aeronautical designers: "Suppose you wanted to invent the airplane, when none had yet been invented, and therefore there were no text books or formulas for doing it. My bet is that you would start— and maybe stop—by leaning on some familiar thing from the past, some precedental concept, as the concept of the bird. But it is plain to see that a bird is built to carry out *many* diverse functions, of which flying may be the *least* important. It is designed to dig holes in the ground or in trees, to eat and digest worms, to build nests, to lay eggs, and so on. (Oh, yes . . . and don't forget that it has to be produced by unskilled labor.) It is amazing how many people there are in aviation today who insist doggedly that the only proper place to put an airplane's wing is on *top* of the body, their only reason being, 'Who ever heard of a low-wing bird!' But, y'know, when those same people want to fly, they don't want to eat worms, too."

To one extent or another, we *all* tend to conceive of things in rigid, fixed, "standard" ways, and to try to bring these old, familiar conceptions to bear upon new problems. Thus, all too commonly, we tend to be led into error and failure by these stereotyped reactions, these "conceptual blocks"—because they channel our thinking narrowly in *old* directions when the problems at hand will yield only to broad, free, imaginative, *new* thinking.

*   *   *

These, then, are twelve strong shackles on our creative imagination. They are not exclusive to you, to me, or to anyone else. They restrict *all* of us in one way or another, to some degree or another, and at some time or another.

*   *   *

Now, here is where I must leave you alone with these inhibitors of Creative Thinking. They are general as to existence; but, being highly variable in their effects and workings within different individuals, they are highly specific and personal where *you* are concerned. Therefore, no matter how earnestly I might *wish* to reveal more to you about the you-ness of them, I am powerless to go beyond the explanations given here. The rest you must do for yourself—in solitary thought and action.

PRACTICAL PRACTICE

This project, carried out fully and faithfully, will produce worthwhile results for you:

1. Review the summary, "Inhibitors of Creative Thinking," on the following pages.
2. Examine yourself in relation to these CT-inhibitors. Check back on your performance(s) and, as carefully as possible, determine how and to what extent each inhibitor tends to influence your performance.
3. Develop as many ideas as you can for alleviating, offsetting or eliminating each of the inhibitors and/or its effects. Put these ideas into practice.
4. Keep on doing "1," "2," and "3," above—not just at this particular time, or while studying the remainder of this book, but for as long as there is value in so doing.

SUMMARY—INHIBITORS OF CREATIVE THINKING

1. *Poor Health:* Physiological and psychological problems —illness, tension, pain, worry, *et al*—intrapersonal problems which interfere with ability to concentrate effectively on the extrapersonal problems of Creative Thinking.
2. *Inadequate Motivation:* Disinterest, indifference, lack of desire to create. (Not necessarily correlated with CT ability/capacity.)
3. *Mental Laziness:* Unwillingness to think. "A characteristic tendency to conserve energy."
4. *Lack of Curiosity:* Unresponsiveness to stimuli. The inability to wonder.

5. *Superficiality:* Shallowness, incompleteness and hastiness of thought, concerned only with the easily apprehended or apparent features of things.

6. *Repressive Training and Education:* Early training and environmental influences that discourage the exercise of natural curiosity and the impulsion to explore and experiment. Educational practices which are essentially information-stuffing processes; which stress the lessons— "Conform! Standardize! Conventionalize!"—which are past-centered; which teach how to imitate, not create.

7. *Job Degradation:* The relegation (including self-relegation) of highly talented people to work that neither permits use of, nor challenges, their mental capacities. The burdening of such people with so much that is "urgent" that they have no time or energy left for what is important. The systematic fractionation and simplification of jobs to the point where they require little more than robot reactions.

8. *Emotion-Mindedness:* "Thalamic thinking." The habit of permitting feelings to distort thinking, encumber reasoning processes, and block objectivity.

9. *Faulty Observation:* Failure to attend. Insensitivity to clues. Obliviousness to evidence—even to the existence of problems. "Inability to see the obvious."

10. *Judicial-Mindedness:* The tendency toward "reflex criticism," toward automatic negative reaction to the new and different. Failure to appreciate that abilities atrophy under fault-finding, flourish under encouragement.

11. *Label-Mindedness:* The habitual tendency to think from the basis of the names of things rather than the facts about them, and thus to be severely limited or misled.

12. *Conceptual Blocks:* Stereotyped reactions; mechanical habits of mind which channel thinking narrowly and fetter the imagination.

Fifth

WHAT ARE THE METHODS?

Of all the information presented in this book up to this point, probably the most important single item is this:

We have all been endowed with Creative Thinking capacity, a mere fraction of which we regularly and habitually use.

As you have seen, the first part of the task of getting more (or all) of our CT potential into greater use is to free ourselves from the inhibitors—poor health, inadequate motivation, mental laziness, lack of curiosity, superficiality, repressive training and education, job degradation, emotion-mindedness, faulty observation, judicial-mindedness, label-mindedness, and conceptual blocks.

The second part of the task of increasing our creativity is to develop *skill* in the use of effective mental methods, processes, systems, procedures, formulas, techniques.

Boiled down, then, the task is two-fold:

1. *Get rid of what's holding us back.*
2. *Get what will push us forward.*

There are a number of "push-forward" CT techniques that have been, and are being, used with success. (Indeed, there are quite a few more than the casual student of CT seems even to have heard of!) I plan to explore *twelve* of them with you here—with some of their main features, applications and limitations.

*　　*　　*

Before you examine any of these techniques, however, you should know this:

First: Strictly speaking, the term "techniques" may not be entirely proper. Some of these methods are so free-wheeling and *non*-technical that it probably would be more appropriate to call them *"approaches."* I will use the former as a standard term; but this is chiefly for the sake of convenience, not exact propriety.

Second: I am not (repeat: *not*) about to "unveil" any sort of "Miracle Formulae" which will "absolutely and automatically," in and of themselves alone, produce one-in-a-million ideas. (Heaven forbid!) The matter isn't that simple. It is not automatic; it is not guaranteed; and, frankly, it is not easy. These techniques are *aids* that can help us to apply our creative ability more efficiently and effectivcly. But they, too, must be *thought* about—examined—experimented with—analyzed—practiced—studied—applied selectively—used intelligently. And above all it must be understood: they are *tools* for easing the mind's work—but they are not the mind.

Now, with this "backdrop" to provide orientation, let's take a look at these twelve *Techniques of Creative Thinking . . .*

I. BRAINSTORMING[1]

One of the simplest and undoubtedly best known techniques of Creative Thinking is called *"Brainstorming."* (Hereinafter I will call it *BS*—with no snide or sinister implications intended, but merely for convenience.)

This technique was developed by Alex F. Osborn, who was one of the co-founders of the highly successful advertising firm of Batten, Barton, Durstine & Osborn. Osborn is the author of what is regarded by many as "the" basic CT text book, *Applied Imagination*. In recent years he has devoted practically full time to the advancement of CT study and education through the non-profit organization, the Creative Education Foundation.

Very simply, Alex Osborn's technique works like this:

First: A *group* meets to do some creative thinking about something. (Mr. Osborn advocates use of the technique by groups of from five to fifteen persons. There are a number of relevant

---

[1] Material adapted from *Applied Imagination*, by Alex F. Osborn. Copyright 1953 and 1957 by Charles Scribner's Sons, 597 Fifth Avenue, New York, N. Y.

refinements, too; and, for information about these, after you have acquired some familiarity here with the fundamentals of the technique, I recommend that you read Mr. Osborn's book and consult the Creative Education Foundation, 1614 Rand Building, Buffalo, N. Y.)

Second: The group proceeds to "think up ideas"—re the subject, of course—in a fast-moving, uninhibited (it is hoped), conference-style manner, observing four "ground rules":

1. *Judicial thinking must be withheld*—until ideation has been carried out. Only after ideation has ceased are overt expressions of judgment, criticism and evaluation permitted.

2. *"Free wheeling" is welcomed.* The "wilder" the ideas, the better—on the principle that a seemingly "wild" idea may suggest a unique revision or "twist" to some other participant who will produce a "tame," "domesticated" or otherwise acceptable version.

3. *Quantity is wanted.* The aim is to produce as many alternatives as possible. The principle underlying this rule is that "Quantity breeds quality"—that is, the greater the number of ideas produced, the greater the likelihood of producing *good* ones. (Long-time users of this technique, after documenting and analyzing their experience, say that, on the average, about six per cent of the ideas produced in BS sessions turn out to be good ones.)

4. *Combination and improvement are sought.* Each participant is expected to suggest how others' proffered ideas can be turned into additional ones.

Third: The group's suggestions are evaluated. This may be done by the group itself or by someone else, according to the circumstances.

As you see, essentially this technique is quite simple. And the "beauty part" of it is: *it works*—when people work it right. (For this reason, perhaps, it has re-awakened the creative spirit in thousands of people in whom this spirit had lain dormant so long that they were willing to believe they were *incapable* of creative thought. If for no other reason than this, Alex F. Osborn has made a tremendous contribution to human benefit!)

Among the variety of BS "success stories" reported are: a sales-winning new package by an aluminum company; an over-the-top Red Feather drive in a western city; an improved public-transportation system in an eastern city; increased blood-donorship in a Veterans Administration hospital; the most popular night-time radio show in a midwestern city; and many others in diverse fields such as government, retailing, public relations and advertising, new products, safety, cost reduction, and so on. And so—on it works.

* * *

At this point, before you read another part of this book, I strongly recommend that you assemble a volunteer CT group and hold some experimental BS sessions. For your first trials, choose some simple, common subjects or aims (*e.g.*, "Name all the uses you can think of to which a burned-out incandescent light bulb might be put"); then—assuming you are the leader—proceed in this fashion:

Step 1: State the subject—as in the "light bulb" suggestion, above.

Step 2: Review the Brainstorming "ground rules" with the members of your group.

Step 3: Elicit group suggestions and record them—quickly, briefly, without comment—on large sheets of paper in plain view of the group. Adhere strictly to the rules. Don't worry about your "leadership technique"; just elicit and record, record and elicit. If the group appears to run short of ideas, try "priming the pump" (to get them going again) by pausing and reviewing aloud the ideas suggested up to this point. Keep going in this way until you are satisfied that the group is "thought out," or there is other reason to stop.

Step 4: Have the group evaluate the ideas.

When you have completed these experimental sessions, and you feel confident of your ability to handle the procedure, go ahead and start to use it "for real." Get a copy of Osborn's book, and study the refinements pertinent to the use of his technique. And, all the while, keep on experimenting with it and thinking about it, to find out how it might be best utilized in the areas of your particular interest(s).

Now, if you have experimented as recommended, no doubt you have discovered that BS *is* a useful and effective technique—within limits. And here, to keep from being bamboozled, you may have to put restraints on your enthusiasm. For this technique is no omnipotent, panacean omnibus.

In truth, there are at least six ways in which BS is inadequate (and maybe even dangerous):

1. *It is designed to get QUICK results, which are not necessarily the best.* And this, of course, is not even possible in dealing with many, many problems requiring Creative Thinking. (Can you imagine *any* group, for example, coming up quickly with "E:mc²"?)

2. *Its effectiveness is confined almost entirely to the treatment of simple, uncomplicated problems.* Successful BS imperatively demands group concentration upon *one* problem, and a simple one at that. Whereas an individual can successfully juggle the multiple components of a complex problem, and still stay on the track, a group is invariably reduced to confused futility when it attempts to brainstorm such a problem.

> Most groups, I find, will never believe this until they personally experience it. So I usually conduct two different BS sessions in point—one on "getting rid of the inhibitor, 'poor health' ", and one on "thinking up uses for the common paper clip." The first session invariably produces a monumental flop and only the most hackneyed of ideas, because the problem is much, much too involved for an ordinary lay group. But the second session practically shoots sparks, and produces genuinely original ideas ("Gee, who would ever have thought an ordinary paper clip . . . !")—and demonstrates the validity of Point #2, above.

Now, this is certainly not to say that a group can not or should not tackle a many-faceted problem, *one sub-problem at a time.* And if your particular group has the tenacity, organization, leadership, mental toughness and discipline to do so, good!—go ahead and try Brainstorming.

3. *By its very "free wheeling" nature, BS is a random, disorganized, planless approach lacking in orderliness and thoroughness.* Thus its promiscuous, *exclusive* use may easily lead to

superficiality, foolish mistakes and "screwball ideas"—the very things you most want to avoid—while the group basks innocently in the mere, illusory *feeling* that it has been "productive."

4. *Successful brainstorming depends upon the group's having broad, related, prior knowledge to bring to bear upon the matter to be BS'd.* This does not mean that the group must be comprised entirely or mostly of experts—which, heaven help us, can sometimes be a terrible *dis*advantage! But, on the other hand, there is no more foolish activity in the field of human endeavor than a BS session on a subject of which the participants have small understanding.

> If you want to see just how futile and ridiculous a group of smart people can be, get a group of such people together and try to BS this assignment: *"Think up all the ideas you can for constructing consonant and dissonant contrapuntal progressions."* Unless your group is made up of specialists—and quite advanced ones, at that—they won't even have a ghost of an idea that the assignment has to do with *music,* let alone have any significant suggestions to offer about "constructing 'whatchamacallits' ".

5. *Brainstorming is a GROUP approach, whereas many (if not most) situations calling for CT are of such nature that INDIVIDUAL handling is necessary.* An informed group may not be available or accessible. The situation may require fast action, with no time to assemble a group. The individual may not be free to divulge the problem at hand to anyone else. The individual may be the only person having adequate knowledge to cope with the problem. The problem may be a complex one requiring extensive, solitary research and study. And, you know, umpity million Frenchmen *can* be wrong, dead wrong, as witness the Maginot Line; and the damages resulting from a group's error generally are much more severe and enduring than in the case of an individual's mistake.

6. *Brainstorming fails to make use of certain operations that are vital to successful Creative Thinking.* (More about these "vital operations" later.) In fact, BS ignores many of these requisites altogether.

Now, just in case you are entertaining some faint suspicion that I have "taken off on BS" here, as for the perverse pleasure of criticizing or some such thing, 'tain't so! I happen to be firmly convinced of the efficacy of this technique—*when it is properly used*. But I have seen too many people plunge into it with insufficient advance study, or jump in with too-high expectations of it, then quickly become disillusioned to the point of rejecting it altogether—thus accomplishing worse than nothing. I see no reason for allowing such a thing to happen to you.

While we're on the subject, I might as well point out that many of the same or similar limitations, misuse-by-people faults, etc., attributed here to BS may also apply to the techniques still to be discussed. It will save time and trouble all around if you will remember this and check for their presence as you go along.

Boiled down, these are probably the points you may find it important to keep foremost in memory about Brainstorming: (1) It is a useful and effective technique. (2) It is an imperfect technique. (3) We should use it judiciously, with understanding of its faults and limitations.

Summary

Brainstorming—An intentionally uninhibited conference-type group approach. Four "ground rules" are observed:

1. Judicial thinking must be withheld—until ideation is carried out.
2. "Free wheeling" is welcomed.
3. Quantity (of ideas) is wanted.
4. Combination and improvement (of ideas) are sought.

The objective is to produce the greatest possible number of alternative ideas for later evaluation and development.

Suggested Brainstorming Exercises

1. Think up all the ideas you can for using a tankful of compressed air.
2. List at least ten ways of supplementing your income without interfering with your regular job.
3. Write down all the ideas you can develop for improving communications in your particular organization.

4. Pick out a number of samples of scrap wherever you work; study these items; and list ways they could be used *other* than as scrap.
5. Imagine that you had a dozen solid-rubber spheres. (Please don't use their common label.) Think of all the things for which you might use them, and list these ideas.
6. Suppose someone gave you 10,000 of "those funny-looking glass things used on telephone poles." List all the uses you can think of for them.
7. Make a list of all the ideas you can think of for cutting down on absenteeism in the organization where you work.
8. Think up all the ideas you can for improving community relations in the city, town or other region where you live.
9. List all the ideas you can think of for getting your boss to give you a raise.
10. Collect ten objects common to your home or business place; then figure out (1) ten ways to improve them, and (2) ten new ways to use them.

II. GORDON TECHNIQUE

Another group approach to CT—one which is less well known than Brainstorming, but which is becoming more widely used as its effectiveness becomes known and appreciated—is called the *"Gordon Technique."*

This technique was developed by William J. J. Gordon, one-time research inventor at the Underwater Sound Laboratory at Harvard University, and more recently head of the "Invention Design Group" of the firm of Arthur D. Little, Incorporated, Cambridge, Massachusetts. ("ADL," or Arthur D. Little, is far from being "addled." It is an outstanding consulting firm which has been unusually successful in performing special services for industrial clients; *e.g.*, solving knotty technical problems and developing new products—developing them, further, from original ideas through to finished products, complete with concomitant manufacturing and marketing plans.)

Independent observers have stated that the Arthur D. Little firm's use of the Gordon Technique has been "importantly responsible" for the firm's consistently high creative output in recent years. So here, evidently, we have a very promising CT method indeed.

And here, now, are the principal features of the Gordon Technique:

First: A group of carefully *selected* people meets to deal with some chosen or assigned problem. According to the nature of the problem and the special knowledges and skills its solution may demand, the group may include artists, engineers, designers, scientists, psychologists, craftsmen, technicians, writers, and just plain highly creative thinkers.

Second: Only the group's *chairman* knows the specific problem to be dealt with. And *the chairman does not reveal the problem to the group* until the group's thinking has advanced to the point where the chairman feels they are getting close to the best solution or solutions.

Third: The chairman leads a broad, *general* group discussion of a subject that is *central* to the problem to be CT'd. For example, the group may be led to discuss . . .

> *"Enjoyment"*—when a new kind of *toy* is sought;
> *"Persuasion"*—to find an improved method of *fishing;*
> *"Opening"*—when the object is to invent a new *can opener;* or
> *"Storing"*—leading to development of a new way to *park cars.*

Throughout the discussion the chairman maintains a permissive, anything-goes kind of attitude. He allows the discussion to move freely, *ad lib,* in whatever directions it may happen to take. And he provides guidance and stimulation chiefly by questioning and by occasionally throwing in significant (but *not* problem-revealing) bits of problem-related information.

Fourth: No maximum time limit is placed on the discussion. Most regular users of the technique, however, find it important to fix some *minimum* time limit—usually about three hours per session—because: (1) fatigue helps to break down certain inhibitors, *e.g.*, fear; which may help to explain why (2) the *best* ideas begin to emerge only after the group *seems* to be "thought out"—that is, to have got the superficial and only-remembered first ideas out of the way—and the members of the group have really *begun* to think creatively.

Fifth: Not only is the time-per-session an important consideration; the *frequency* of these sessions has also been found to be important. Most people having had extensive experience with the Gordon Technique agree that the three-hour-plus meetings are usually so exhausting (and sometimes so over-exciting) that it is inadvisable to hold them any more often than once a week.

Sixth: When, in a given session, the group seems to be getting close to a good solution for the problem at hand, the chairman finally reveals all of the particulars of the problem. From this point on, then, the principle behind the problem-solution is crystallized, and the group starts to develop the idea in detail. They do not seek a multitude of general alternatives or "possibilities" as an end, as is usually the case with the Brainstorming technique. Rather, they seek the one or two *best* ideas—which they then follow through to completion.

*   *   *

At this point, it will pay you to assemble another volunteer group, as in the previous Brainstorming-practice meeting, and try a CT session using the Gordon Technique. When your group is ready, Mister Chairman, proceed in this fashion:

> *Step 1:* Announce the subject as *"Separating."* (Actually you are going to try to get the group to create a new lawn-mowing device—or, at least, to conceive of a new *principle* for one. But whatever you do, don't tell them so, or use the terms "grass cutting" or "lawn mowing," else you'll wind up brainstorming, not "Gordonizing.")
>
> *Step 2:* Elicit from the group all the ideas they can think of for *ways of separating things.* (Don't try to prevent them from thinking in terms of "sorting," "filing," "coding," etc.— not at first, at least—but let them go along whatever lines they will.) Record the suggestions on large sheets of paper in the view of the group. As you make progress, gradually "feed" essential bits of information to the group ("We are seeking ways to separate solid objects from themselves, as it were . . . Each is variable in length; say, from three to five inches; and

we want to retain one inch . . .") until you feel that they have exhausted most of the possibilities and have conceived of basic principles which can lead to development of original, unique solutions for the problem.

If your group performs as most groups do, you will find at this stage that they have suggested a yard-long list of general "ways of separating things," including . . .

burning	implosion	decomposition
exploding	pulling	hydraulic streams
corrosion	magnetism	chemical action
breaking	centrifuging	sand blasting
friction	jet action	atomic radiation
chewing	precipitating	ultrasonic waves

. . . and so on and on and on.

This is the stage, then, at which to begin moving from the general to the specific. ("The material in our problem is a kind of fibrous ribbon—a little like paper—one end of each piece of which is held firmly in fixed position. . . . The ribbons are closely spaced on a relatively flat plane which may be horizontal, slanted, etc. . . . Knowing this, and the object of our effort, which of the general forces listed could you possibly employ, and how would you use them?") Keep going in this way until you feel that your group is on the trail of one or more basic ideas for solving the problem in genuinely unique but sound fashion.

Step 3: Reveal the full problem to the group (*still* in terms of "separating blades of grass from themselves," *not* in terms of "cutting" or "mowing") and guide the ensuing discussion toward development of specific ideas for applying the principles previously elicited and recorded. ("You say, 'Use a rapidly vibrating wire—a kind of ultrasonic piano wire. . . .' How would you power or drive it? What would the machine look like?" And so on.) Record these new suggestions separately, with sketches as needed.

Step 4: Continue as described in the preceding text, according to the requirements of your particular situation. (It will be impractical, of course, to carry this practice session to the extreme of *actually* trying to develop any of the group's ideas in detail—unless by sheer coincidence this *is* a real problem to you. But there are obvious benefits to be derived from discussion of this step.)

I believe you will find that successful application of the Gordon Technique makes heavier demands upon both the chairman and the group than does the simpler Brainstorming technique—and, therefore, that considerably more practice may be needed before you will feel confident about applying it to real-life problems. Accordingly, I have provided some additional suggested practice problems for you at the end of this section.

*   *   *

Perhaps the most important general information to keep in mind, relative to the effective use of the Gordon Technique, is this:

It seems to work best in thinking up ideas for *products*—for tangible things. (This tentative conclusion derives mostly from the observation that its most extensive and successful use to date appears to have been in connection with tangibles. Experimental evidence, however, indicates that it may be used with equal effectiveness in dealing with certain intangibles.)

Its effective use requires a highly skilled, stimulating *leader,* one who is himself a highly qualified and highly creative person.

It requires a carefully selected *group,* the members of which have been chosen after consideration of special qualifications as to background, training, knowledge, temperament and skill.

It requires a group of people who are compatible and who will work together unselfishly and in good spirit toward *group* goals.

*   *   *

Personally, I am quite "high" on the Gordon Technique, for these four main reasons:

1. It automatically blocks-out certain CT inhibitors (label-

mindedness, emotion-mindedness, etc.) and forces objective consideration of underlying, basic *principles,* thereby achieving the most salutary effect of driving a wedge into the mind and opening-up the imagination to possibilities that otherwise would not be explored.

2. It avoids/averts/obviates "egocentric involvement" (a common hazard in most conference-type approaches)—that is, the tendency of participants to attach personal, possessive feelings to their own particular ideas, to over-defend them, to "protect" them, etc. (After a group has been occupied for some time in a Gordon-Technique session, they find that they not only don't care who contributed what ideas; they can't even *remember* who did, even if it should be important to do so.)

3. It avoids/averts/obviates superficiality—"solutions too soon arrived at," William Gordon puts it—and fosters thoroughness and depth of thought.

4. It tends to compel follow-through to testing and verification of the ideas produced.

Summary

Gordon Technique—A variation of brainstorming with these main features:

1. The chairman leads a *general* group discussion on a subject which is *central* to the problem to be solved.
2. The chairman does not reveal the specific problem-assignment until he feels that the group is getting close to a satisfactory solution.
3. The group has a free discussion, with the chairman guiding, questioning, and occasionally supplying problem-related information.
4. When the group seems close to a good solution, the chairman reveals the specific problem—whereupon the principle behind the solution is crystallized, and the group then develops the idea in detail.

The objective usually is to produce *one* best idea, and to carry it through to testing, verification, development, and production in final form.

Suggested Gordon-Technique Exercises

Subject . . .   *Object: Develop a new . . .*
"Safety" ....lock.
"Pleasure" ....game or sport.
"Black & White" ....printing process.
"Temperature" ......insulating method.
"Shape" ....company trademark.
"Energy" ....power source or fuel.
"Space/Place" ....method of navigation.
"Removing" ....method of opening packages.
"Attraction" ....advertising method or device.
"Level" ....method for "ironing" clothes.
"Together" ....book-binding device or method.
"Force" ....propulsion system for vehicles.
"Separating" ....method of cleaning or removing dirt.

A DIGRESSION FOR TOGETHERNESS/EXPERTNESS

Well, they have already started—the uncertainties; the unclarities; the seemingly contradictory evidences; the foggy implications, nuances, inferences, innuendoes, conclusions; the apparently conflicting fundamental theses . . .

In one paragraph/breath, some fellow (who, me?) says that having a CT group "comprised . . . of experts . . . can . . . be a terrible disadvantage"—the obvious (?) conclusion being, therefore, that having a CT group made up of amateurs is *de rigueur*. But in almost the next paragraph/breath this same fellow says that "a carefully *selected* group . . . of . . . artists, engineers, designers, scientists, psychologists" is the thing—and just how expert can you get?!

In still another place it is made quite clear that *group* action is what it takes to get creative results. Yet, practically cheek-to-cheek with this glad tiding is the happy little note that there are at least a half-dozen solid reasons why only *individual* thinking will do.

And if one will trouble himself some time to attend any of the increasingly common regional/national conferences on creativity, chances are he will find there that some harried program chairman, desperate for ways to put a little life into the proceedings, will have got together a panel of protagonists who will shortly have at it . . .

"Group thinking is no damn good!"

"It is, too, some damn good!"

"The professor at Yale says . . ."

"He didn't use the approved method."

"But Alex has shown . . ."

"Not according to Zilboorg!"

. . . And around and 'round it goes, generating high heat and little light.

And where does all this leave the poor guy who has no interest whatever in raging controversies but simply wants to know whether—with *his* particular qualifications and *his* particular situation—he should proceed one way or another? Well, not only must it leave him, to quote a certain earthy friend, ". . . as confused as the little boy who dropped his chew o' gum in the chicken coop," but it must make him feel like chucking the whole frenetic, fustian foolishness and going back to making buggy whips. (Y' blame him?)

But we can't have any such thing happening to *you*. You've come too far already. You've spent hard-earned money (*some-body's*) and expensive time to get this far. And, very simply, you deserve better. So, if you don't mind digressing from the methods-and-techniques exposition for a while, let's look into these matters a little deeper and see if we can finally settle the dust on them in a constructive way.

*   *   *

First, the matter of togetherness . . .

It has been quite fashionable in recent years to believe that:

(1) to make rapid, fundamental progress in solving any given problem, it is necessary only to commit large numbers of men and dollars to the task of solving the problem; and,

(2) in these days of mass organizations, general conformity

and subordinated individuals, invention is a systematic process which can be carried forward effectively only by great teams (nay, armies!) of trained technicians and specialists, and the day of the "loner," the Thomas-Edison-at-Menlo-Park, is dead as the dodo.

The first of these propositions can be disposed of rather quickly. It is based on the premise that, if two men can pick a ton of apples a day, four men can pick two tons; therefore: if one man can produce a new invention in a year, two men can do it in six months. And there is one thing very badly wrong with this "logic": it is spurious; if one man can produce an invention in a year, two men may require *two* years—or 22—or *forever*. There is no standard determination of how long it takes to get an idea.

It throws no light on the matter to cite the cases of Manhattan-Project-and-The-Bomb, and the post-Sputnik "crash program," either. For even the most cursory investigation will show that the nuclear scientists and the rocketeers—the Einsteins and Fermis and Goddards and von Brauns—were *privately* at work on the relevant fundamental problems for years and years before they finally got (or could even have used!) all of the hardware, facilities, implementation and other *developmental* aids needed for the final integration/perfection of their inventions.

Now, let's make no mistake about this. Great gobs of money, material and manpower were indispensable to the finishing of these monumental creative efforts. But these "great gobs" were *not* in themselves originative, not primarily causative.

The second of the foregoing propositions—the one about team *vs.* solo invention—shouldn't take long, either.

In a comprehensive, thoroughly documented study sponsored recently by the Rockefeller Foundation, Professor John Jewkes and his assistants, David Sawers and Richard Stillerman, have concluded—only after the most exhaustive investigation, remember—that the individual inventor, working alone in his workshop, is indisputably "the winner and *still* world champion" in turning out new discoveries and inventions.* After looking into the origins of sixty major inventions produced since the year

---

* The Jewkes-Sawers-Stillerman study has been published as *The Sources of Invention,* by St. Martin's Press, 175 Fifth Avenue, New York, N. Y.

1900, *i.e.*, spanning the era of the large modern industrial-research organizations, Professor Jewkes' group found this: twenty-one of these inventions came from the big research organizations; six could not be satisfactorily classified; and *thirty-three* of them came from *individual* contributors.

Among the inventions credited to the "mass-production labs" were: Duco lacquers, nylon, fluorescent lighting, polyethylene, cellophane, DDT, the diesel-electric locomotive, and silicones.

Among the inventions credited to the "loners": chromium plating, automatic transmission for automobiles, radio, penicillin, the electron microscope, insulin, the self-winding wrist watch, the gyrocompass, the slide fastener ("zipper"), streptomycin, the gas refrigerator for homes, quick-freezing, and the helicopter.

It would be absurd to try to minimize the importance of the modern laboratory, with its organized research methods and facilities. (Can you cite anything better for efficiently processing and utilizing the astronomical quantities and varieties of facts about our universe?) But it would be just as absurd to fail to see that the individual has contributed as much, and probably more, to human progress than the "assembly liners." And it would be the very height of absurdity to fail to recognize that *ideas originate in human brains*—which may or may not be housed concurrently in laboratories or other "creative" work-shops, and which may or may not be in close, frequent communication with others of like kind.

*   *   *

Second, the matter of expertness . . .

Copernicus was expert only in medicine and canon law, but founded modern astronomy. Pasteur, a chemist, not a doctor, produced the germ theory of disease. Edison, with no formal training at all as a scientist, gave us a whole series of important scientific inventions.

"Ancient history!" you say? All right . . .

An amateur "science buff" named John Campbell suggested that our government use lithium hydride rather than tritium as the fuel for our first hydrogen bomb, because tritium would be hard to handle and would be enormously expensive to produce. But the AEC went ahead with tritium, and in 1952 exploded a hydrogen device, the development of which cost three billion dollars. The Russians, using the fuel our amateur suggested, later developed their own hydrogen bomb, and it is reported to have cost twenty million dollars—or *$2,980,000,000 less than ours!*

And one of America's most advanced aeronautical firms recently invested thousands and thousands of dollars, several years of research by top scientists, and the use of highly "sophisticated" machines and facilities to build a wheel-less vehicle—a GEM, or Ground Effect Machine—that would float on air and skim along on a "ground cushion" of air just above the earth's surface. An "average" Alaskan high school boy, 17-year-old Craig Vetter, accomplished the same thing—with spare time, a five-horsepower chain-saw engine, some plywood, an old tractor fan, some miscellaneous junk, and a total cash investment of four dollars!

Does this mean that "experts are no good" as innovators? Of course not! It means that *both* experts and amateurs *can* be good innovators.

Without going into tedious detail: the evidence seems to indicate that the expert is generally far more (and indispensably) proficient at *development* than at origination of real breakthroughs. He knows *too* much about what *has been* done and what *has been* tried unsuccessfully in his field. He is too habituated to thinking along established lines to be able to innovate easily, although seemingly having "every advantage."

The amateur, on the other hand, while ostensibly less well equipped, may actually hold the real advantage—at least in the respect that he is supposedly too dumb to know that a thing can't be done, so goes ahead and does it. As though to offset this, however and unhappily, the amateur has to face the obstacle that just about *everyone* "knows" more about his chosen field of attempted innovation than he does; so ... (You do recall, of course, that you were warned at the outset: "Only men, not boys, need apply" for CT work?)

* * *

And now, after all this, what do you conclude? (Unavoidably, you understand, you *will* have to decide finally for yourself.) Personally, I suspect that the indicated conclusions may read like this:

• Any one person who wants to create new ideas has more

reasons to believe he can do so than reasons to believe he can not do so.

- Twelve guys may add up twelve times dumber than one guy.
- Groups may provide several things, including: (1) stimulation; (2) exchanges of information, sometimes supplying missing links in chains of information, thus making possible the final integration of complex *continua;* (3) influence on attitudes; (4) the comfort of numbers; (5) sociability. And some of these may contribute to CT.
- Twelve thinkers may just think the same thought twelve times.
- If you stop to confer, don't forget to go back to work afterward.
- Ideas have no pride—they are willing to be born to anyone willing to bear them.
- Ideas occur to individuals—who are sometimes expert, sometimes not; sometimes alone, sometimes not—and the ideas don't give a whoop in Wapakoneta *which* they are.

*   *   *

III. Attribute Listing

Possibly one of the oldest formal techniques of Creative Thinking—certainly one of the oldest that has been generally recognized, regarded and taught as such—is the one originated and taught at the University of Nebraska by Professor Robert P. Crawford. (It should also be noted that Dr. Crawford's book, *The Techniques of Creative Thinking,* has come to be accepted as one of the standard CT works.) The technique which Professor Crawford formulated, and which has been an important part of the highly successful classes he has taught since 1931, is called—*"Attribute Listing."*

A highly effective if basically simple technique, Attribute Listing can be and is used both by groups and by individuals working alone. And while its usefulness is not necessarily confined to this application, it is most commonly used for *improving tangible things.*

The philosophical "heart" or rationale of Professor Crawford's technique might be summed up in two fundamental findings:

First: Everything starts from something else. Everything—at least, in *homo sapien's* field of operations—starts from the present state or set of conditions, from the-thing-as-it-is-here-and-now, from the-up-to-now, from the-matter-at-the-moment, from the *status quo*. Thus, according to Crawford's thesis, every new idea begins not from scratch but from "something old . . . borrowed . . ."

Second: Creation equals observation plus adaptation of that which is observed. Thus, a new idea is simply an old one to which something has happened—or, rather, to which something is *made* to happen—a present being which is noted, then changed.

To transpose from the philosophical to the operational, now: the essential application of the Attribute Listing technique consists of carrying out four main steps:

Step 1: Choose something to improve. And what might this be? Anything, practically. Choose the first thing you see as you look around, if you wish. But, if possible, try to choose something that you care about, that is important to you, that interests you. (Certainly, you can work effectively on something about which you are only lukewarm, or which is assigned to you without much regard for your wishes! *C'est la vie, non?* But you are most likely to get really dedicated to that to which you *want* to be dedicated.)

Step 2: List the parts of the product. This is to keep you from overlooking key elements of your problem/product during succeeding steps.

Step 3: List the essential, basic qualities, features or attributes of the parts and/or the whole product. That is, *describe* the product. List its distinguishing features—the features that make the product distinctive, interesting, valuable, operable. Describe it in terms of its important characteristics or properties. For example, if the object chosen for improvement were, say, the common lead pencil, some of the pertinent descriptive phrases might be: ". . . wood shaft, ¼ x 7½ inches . . . hexagonal cross-section . . . red rubber eraser on one end . . . tapered round lead . . ." etc.

Step 4: Systematically change or modify the attributes to better-satisfy the original purpose of the product or to satisfy a new need with it. Do you need a "for-instance"? If the object is long—make it short; make it longer . . . If the object is straight—coil it; make it curved; corrugate it . . . And so on.

*   *   *

Do you have the four steps in mind, now? Perhaps you had better review them, to clarify them. Then try your hand at applying them by completing this exercise:

Step 1: Choose the *common picture frame* to improve.

Step 2: "List the parts . . ." Jot down: (a) *frame,* (b) *front cover,* (c) *back cover,* (d) *hanging devices.* (Since this is only an illustrative exercise, omit the picture itself and small items such as the hooks and fasteners, etc. In dealing with your real problems, however, you should consider any such items even though at the moment they might seem to be of "only minor importance." By the way, the purpose of this step is to help to keep you from overlooking important attributes; thus, it is more a preparatory than a "working" step.)

Step 3: List the following attributes as headings on a separate sheet of paper: (a) *rectangular shape,* (b) *glass front,* (c) *wooden frame,* (d) *back-opening,* (e) *hangs by wire.*

Step 4: "Systematically change . . ." Now create ideas: think about one attribute at a time, and systematically change or modify it in your mind, making notes on the changes as you go along. (E.g.: The *shape* could be *oval, three-dimensional,* etc. The *front* could be *plastic, mesh,* etc. The *frame* could be of *metal, paper,* etc. The *opening* could be at the *side* or *top.* The whole assembly could be *held up* by *suction cups, magnets,* etc.) Follow on out in this way just as far as you possibly can. Then check and see—how many possible combinations did you come up with?

When you have completed this exercise, thought about it, and found how easily this technique works, go right ahead and start using Attribute Listing in real projects where its use is appropriate. Naturally, you would be wise to study Professor Crawford's book, too. But you need not wait for a complete digestion of his book to begin making use of his CT technique.

*   *   *

It is obvious, of course, that the ideas developed through the use of Attribute Listing should (must!) be tested, verified, judged, evaluated—*after* the ideas have been produced. (This is true where other techniques are used, too; so, if you are agreeable, let's save ourselves time, space and effort from this point forward by accepting this as an implicitly understood standard step in the use of *every* CT technique.)

If there is any particular pitfall to be wary of in connection with Attribute Listing—other than those carried over implicitly from other techniques, that is—it may be this:

Attribute Listing works with such simple, effective ease that you may be inclined to react, "It's too good to be true." To which I can only respond: Doggone it, it *is* simple and easy and effective! It is so much so, in fact, that I am going to refrain from suggesting any pertinent practice exercises at all, and simply repeat—*start using the Attribute Listing technique in projects where its use is appropriate.*

Summary

Attribute Listing—A technique used chiefly for *improving* tangible things. Procedure:

1. Choose some object to improve.
2. List the parts of the object.
3. List the essential, basic qualities, features or attributes of the object and its parts.
4. Systematically change or modify the attributes.

The objective is to better-satisfy the original purpose of the object, or to fulfill a new need with it.

IV. Input-Output Technique

One of America's most important industrial organizations has for a number of years conducted an internal course in "Creative Engineering" for its technical personnel. According to published statements, the graduates of this course consistently produce several times as many patentable ideas and new processes as do the non-graduates. And one of the major factors contributing to this conspicuous success is believed to be the use of the so-called *"Input-Output Technique"* of CT.

The Input-Output Technique was developed originally as *a method for solving dynamic-system design problems*—that is, a method for solving problems in the design of various and sundry devices, contrivances and apparatuses for performing physical work.

The technique derives its name from the observation that a dynamic system can be classified according to its . . .

> *Input*—ingoing power or force.
> *Output*—corresponding action or reaction.
> *Specifications*—or limiting requirements.

For example, in designing *an automatic device for shading a room during bright sunlight,* the problem might be defined as follows:

> *Input*—solar energy: heat and light.
> *Output*—make windows alternately opaque and transparent.
> *Specifications*—the system must . . .
>   (a) be usable on various-size windows;
>   (b) admit no more than 20 foot-candle illumination anywhere in the room; and
>   (c) cost less than $100 per 40-square-foot window.

Once the problem has been defined in terms of these three factors, the object becomes that of finding means to *bridge the gap between input and output.* This is done principally by asking oneself repeatedly, "How can this particular 'input' be used (preferably as directly as possible) to bring about the desired 'output'?"—then answering oneself with all of the alternatives that can be brought to mind.

In the case of our hypothetical room-shading-device problem, for example, the questioning and answering might proceed something like this:

> *Q:* What is there that reacts/responds to solar heat and light?
> *A:* There may be vapors that cloud . . .
>   Gases and metals expand . . .
>   Glass reflects, refracts . . .
>   Solids soften or melt . . .
>   Plants move, grow . . .

Photo-electric cells produce current . . .

Chemicals change . . .

Fuel cells convert chemical energy . . .

Solar batteries . . .

Q: Can any of these be used directly to shade the window?

A: Possibly chemicals or vaporous materials that cloud when they are heated or exposed to light . . .

Bi-metals warp; so perhaps they could be used in a blind, the slats of which would warp shut . . .

Expanding gas could operate bellows . . .

Heat effect on the electrical conductivity of metals might be utilized . . .

Photo-electric current could operate a solenoid . . .

The panes might possibly be tilted automatically in some relation to refraction . . .

Bellows could operate a blind . . .

There are a number of ways of actuating motors to draw blinds or drapes . . .

A kind of plant life might be found or developed . . .

In this manner, as you can see, a number of possible solutions can be explored. Each one, in turn, can then be tested and evaluated, and the best one or ones selected for "the full treatment."

The Input-Output Technique intrinsically has a number of advantages similar to those of the Gordon Technique. And experimental evidence indicates that, when it is modified slightly so as to permit use in the same general manner as the Gordon Technique—that is, as a group technique, with the initial discussion concentrated upon the subject of the *input,* and a similar but separate discussion focused upon the *output*—its effectiveness may be even further increased.

*Summary**

Input-Output Technique—A method for solving dynamic-system design problems. Procedure:

---

* For a detailed and authoritative exposition of many of the important particulars related to the Input-Output Technique, see *Professional Creativity,* by E. K. Von Fange; Prentice-Hall, Inc.; 1959.

1. Specify the *input*—the power or force going into the system.
2. Specify the *output*—the corresponding action or reaction desired.
3. Define the limiting requirements or specifications.
4. Bridge the gap between input and output—find ways to make the input produce the desired output within the specified limitations.

The objective is to produce a number of possible solutions which can then be tested, evaluated and developed.

Suggested Input-Output Technique Exercises

The Input-Output Technique is one that may be clarified more by practice than by verbalization. And, to make your practice of the use of this technique especially productive, I suggest that you proceed in this way:

1. From the list of "Inputs" and "Outputs," below, choose one of each at random.

Inputs		Outputs	
Sound	Magnetism	Keep Time	Mix or Blend
Explosion	Vacuum	Move Fluids	Shape Metal
Sunlight	Gravity	Cook Foods	Action Toy
Water Flow	Radiation	Transport	Lift Objects
Compression	Moving Air	Entertain	Wash or Clean

2. Apply the Input-Output Technique to these randomly-matched items in the same manner as in the case of the automatic-room-shading-device example in the preceding text.

3. Continue as above until it seems to have become natural to use the Input-Output Technique. (Since there are 10 input-items and the same number of output-items here, you have 100 possible exercises.) And when that "comes-natural" feeling occurs—there's your signal, loud and clear, to start using the technique on your "for-keeps" problems.

V. CATALOG TECHNIQUE

One of the very simplest (and therefore workable?) of the recognized techniques of Creative Thinking is so very simple that it hardly seems to merit the dignity of the term, "technique." But when we begin to see and appreciate its efficiency and efficacy, the question of nominal propriety quickly fades into unimportance. This technique is called the *"Catalog Technique."*

As its name may suggest, the Catalog Technique consists of nothing more complicated (procedurally, at least) than *consulting some kind of catalog as a means of getting ideas that will, in turn, suggest other ideas.* That is, it is a practical way of applying one of the basic CT principles mentioned earlier ("Everything starts from something else")—of reviewing already-known information and ideas for hints or clues to the yet-unknown—of making direct use of the old to build the new. For instance . . .

Do you want to write a better letter—one that isn't just another repetition of the same tired, hackneyed phrases in your previous letter, and the one before that, and the one before that, and so on? Then try consulting a thesaurus: a dictionary of synonyms and antonyms. It may quickly help you to exchange drab phraseology like "excessively wordy television commercial messages" for a more colorful kind such as "bombastic boob-tube blurbs"—and have a little new fun in the process.

Do you want to make a "Work Sampling" study as a basis upon which to formulate certain management decisions in your company? To make a reliable one, you will need some way to insure the randomness of your pertinent observation-checks. A catalog of random numbers will shorten this task measurably—and possibly lead to unexpected new values, as well.

Do you want to invent a new name for a new baby? You might start by consulting one of the books of names, then re-spelling ("Dru" instead of "Drew"?), or combining/coining ("Druann" for Andrew's new daughter?) or you-name-it—literally.

Do you want to find some products that your packaging company could put up advantageously in paperboard cartons? A look-see into one of the famous American mail-order catalogs could be *just* the starting place.

Do you want to design a certain tool or machine part? (*Now* it's out—one of the most carefully guarded secrets of "practical-ahem!" engineering:) Consult those certain (nameless) catalogs, then; and observe that depicted therein is a thing which, changed just thus-and-so, or modified just so-and-thus . . . *Voila*—a new creation! And it *will* be a new creation, too, if only it is not *quite* like anything else of its general kind. (By the bye: if you should refer to a parts catalog and find that the exact part you're seeking —or a better one—has already been created, this isn't exactly a loss, is it?)

Do you want to give a speech on creativity? (Oh, you poor soul! Where does it seem to hurt the most?) Well, if you can't get out of it before the programs are printed, then by all means check into some book of quotations and see if it is really true that Albert Einstein may be quoted as saying, "Imagination is more important than knowledge." And if the quotation is correct, ask yourself: why on earth did he say that; what did he mean? And see if this doesn't lead to the development of a much-more-interesting-than-usual talk. Betcha!

What else do you want to accomplish in creative manner? Whatever it may be, see if any of the following types of catalogs might be useful (and jot down marginal notes and notes about additional kinds of catalogs too, hmmm?):

Cook Books _____
"Who's Who" _____
Encyclopedia _____
Case Histories _____
Newspaper "Morgues" _____
"Word/Phrase Finders" _____
Rhyming Dictionaries _____
Business Directories _____
Professional Abstracts _____
Seed or Botanical Catalogs _____
_____
_____
_____

By the way, just in case you missed the point, let's spell it out: Use of the Catalog Technique never, *never* means copying! It means using presently known ideas as "ticklers" to give general suggestions as to adaptations, modifications, etc., that may lead to the development of *new* ideas.

But you still have "faint twinges of conscience," you say? Then you must not understand; so let's back up jus-s-t a bit: CT does not demand utter, complete, total newness. (Didn't we dispel this false notion of absolute novelty and gigantism long ago, incidentally?) On the contrary (almost), the demand is more for variation than revolution. Furthermore, using the Catalog Technique is simply systematizing and extending what one does naturally in CT anyhow—that is, search (usually only in limited memory, as it happens) for "something to tie to," for a springboard, for something to "strike sparks" to get the CT machinery going. So you see, Virginia, it is perfectly legitimate . . .

In some situations, the Catalog Technique may be used directly, as a fully "accredited" technique in its own right. In others, it may be used as an adjunct to other methods. But in any case, you are likely to find that it so streamlines and simplifies certain phases of the CT job that you will sometimes feel, "Now, why on earth didn't I think of that before?!"

Summary

Catalog Technique—Simply the reference to various and sundry catalogs as a means of getting ideas that will, in turn, suggest other ideas.

VI. FREE ASSOCIATION

". . . association . . . society . . . people . . . by for at who with from to . . . group family folks loner . . . loneliness of thought dreariness of work . . . quote unquote . . . black white red green . . . rich blue white . . . Piper Comanche 180! . . . four thousand feet south southwest lock haven nittany tussey mountain spruce creek valley . . . clean beautiful loop martinsburg quilt patches . . . glorious shades tones hues . . . hews . . . woods pennsylvania penns woods . . . sylvania electric wood nonconductor . . . why ear itch guyton grizzy . . . uhhh fooll . . . 'griseofulvin'! . . . ask guyton prescription fixed dog . . . dog ear . . . curled paper flatten print smooth . . . waste down quality up . . . customers reputation corporate image glamorous name . . . glamorous what women want . . . women switch to save nickel . . . *'nickelsaver' ads promotion sales* . . . That's it, that's it—we'll have 'Nickel-Saver Sales,' NSS Days!"

"Now, what in the name of something-or-other is *that?*" you say? "Gibberish from Ward Eight? Some puckish printer, using up all his old type, or sumpin'?" Not at all. *"That,"* dear student of CT, is a small sample of a *thought-stream*:* an illustration, as it happens, of one of the most-significant-to-CT of all human phenomena—namely, the phenomenon of *free association.*

And what is "free association"? It is a process wherein, basically, from some starting point ("everything" *still* "starts from something else") the mind recalls one experience, image, symbol or bit of information—and this leads to the recall of another experience, image, symbol or bit of information—*etc., ad lib, ad infinitum.* It is a process in which the mind "hauls" one recollection after another before the consciousness for "inspection," as it were—in halting, stop-and-go fashion—with no apparent directional intent or conscious volition or guidance—until, in effect, the mind "recognizes" or takes cognizance of something; or comes alert/awake; or forms a sort of "Hey!" response/awareness; or, simply, something "registers."

There is at least one school of thought in psychology that defines thinking as "a sequential arousal of symbols." Which is a kind of economical way of expressing three pertinent ideas:

1. One thing leads to another: something occurs to us; this reminds us of something else; and this of still another thing; and so on.
2. Thinking is mostly a matter of digging up, arranging and rearranging memories.
3. "1" and "2," above, ordinarily occur pretty much at random.

Now, personally, I am not quite ready to accept this as an adequate definition: that the mere, willy-nilly matching of memories may, in fact, *be* thinking—or what passes for thinking with most of us. (Are we only animate EDP machines?) But I *am* willing to go on record with *this* conclusion: Anyone with a little capacity for self-discipline can readily, habitually and systematically give the essential process of free association such direc-

---

* It is apparent, of course, that this verbal presentation is, and can be, only a partial representation of the flow of symbols through a mind; that many related sensations and concomitant feelings are missing.

tion, impetus and control as to constitute the degree implicit in the concept of a deliberate, rational technique; a wide-awake scheme, structure, procedure; a volitional plan, program or method.

And therein is the whole point of this discussion, so far as organized Creative Thinking is concerned.

There are really at least *two* fundamental free-association processes:

There is an *unstructured* one (with small-case letters) wherein the mind simply starts wherever it happens to "be" at a given moment, then drifts along freely, as in our opening paragraph, until it gets "somewhere." This is the one that underlies such so-called CT techniques as Brainstorming and the Catalog Technique; *i.e.*, it is what explains these others, what makes them work.

And there is a *structured* one (with capital letters) wherein the mind is, in effect, presented with a carefully selected starting symbol-of-origin, a symbol having key relevance to the problem at hand, then proceeds in some *non*-irrelevant manner toward some fairly definite goal. This latter process is a CT entity in itself—a "fully accredited" CT technique in its own right. And how does this second, or directed, process work?

Assuming that one has already thought of something to "think up" *about*, the applied CT principle/technique of Free Association works like this:

Step 1: Jot down a symbol—a symbol that is related in some *key* way to some important aspect of the subject/problem under consideration. This symbol may be a *word*, a *sketch*, a *number*, a *picture*, or whatever; but it must be *centrally related to the subject* at hand.

Step 2: Jot down a symbol suggested by the first one. Don't try to concentrate or to "think about it." Just record whatever comes to mind—idly, as though you are merely musing and care not one whit whether you are being productive, constructive, "going in the right direction," or anything else, especially.*

It is a little awkward to interrupt the presentation of steps in

---

* Note the use of the verb, "record", above. It suggests a variation in procedure wherein one does not write but, rather, speaks into a voice-recording machine. If you have access to such equipment, by all means use it; it may work to excellent advantage for you.

this way, but I believe you'll find the whole explanation clearer for the doing. So, if you will, stop reading text at this point, and carry out this exercise:

1. Get a sheet of paper and write the word-symbol, *"SHON,"* at the top of the sheet.
2. Allow yourself one minute in which to free-associate from this starting symbol and, as explained in Step 2, to write down whatever comes to mind. Start *now*.
3. Stop at the end of one minute; then count the symbols you have written.

Now, if your list of "SHON"-associated symbols numbers only 10 or so, you are not yet into the swing of it. So you had better take another minute and free-associate some more—and this time, as the old song puts it, let yourself go!

And just what does this exercise prove, if anything? At the moment I am trying to show only that your mind *will* associate freely—as another old songs says, by "doin' what comes natcherly." There is no special knack, trick or new technique involved at this point. The only real knack comes in *letting* your mind do what it will do naturally, without any special direction (if, so to speak, you will "give it its head"), and then *later* capitalizing on its output, as will be explained in connection with Step 3.

Before you go on to Step 3, however, it might be wise to choose one or two new symbols at random—anything at all, such as the first thing you see, or see implied, if you pause here and look up—and get some more practice in performing this kind of "productive day dreaming."

Step 3: Continue Step 2—ad lib—until ideas emerge. Continue until some of the symbols you have recorded "jump out" at you or in some way make a "special" impression that leads to the kind of ideas you are seeking. If this does not seem to occur naturally, even though you have continued to associate freely for a considerable time, stop; then deliberately review and analyze your record of symbols, select those that seem to have some special implications in relation to your subject/problem, and re-work or adapt or modify them as seems necessary to fit them to the purpose you are trying to accomplish.

For Instance . . .

Is this "clear as mud"? Then let's clarify it by applying the steps in their entirety to a life-like situation.

Borrowing a suggestion from the Gordon Technique, I will

withhold the underlying problem for the moment and simply recommend that, for the next five minutes, you apply the Free Association technique to this word-symbol: *"CLEAN."*

Go ahead, now—with Steps 1 and 2—for the next five minutes.

Five minutes up? All right. If you have really worked at recording whatever came to mind relative to the word-symbol, "Clean," you have listed at least 50 associated symbols. So now, with these, apply Step 3:

The problem—Imagine that you have developed a new kind of cleaning agent (soap or detergent) which is as yet unnamed.

The aim—Think up a name for your product.

The procedure—Review the symbols you have listed in association with the key symbol, "Clean," and develop possible names from them. (*E.g.:* If one of the symbols you have listed is the word, *"sunny,"* this might suggest to you the name, *"Sunny Suds."* Or, if you have the symbol, *"bright,"* you might re-spell it as *"Brite."*) Continue until you have worked out at least 25 possible new names for your hypothetical new product.

And For Instance . . .

Want to try another practice exercise? Good! Imagine that you have the job of preparing a one-page newspaper advertisement for the *Forrest City Lumber Company*. So . . .

for	rest	for the rest of your life	four good reasons
four	for	forest for the trees	four backwards is ruof
numeral 4		regular 4 and backwards 4 together look like a tree	

(Go ahead and carry this on out . . .)

And a Different For-Instance . . .

Artist "Eddie" Pirman executed one of the most striking designs I have ever seen when he started from the symbols . . .

circle—for an operation; *square*—for an inspection; *triangle* —for a storage; *arrow*—for a transportation; *"D"*—for delay

. . . then leaned back, studied the symbols intently for a moment, grasped paper and pencil, and in *minutes* created the unique Methods Improvement Manual cover design shown here:

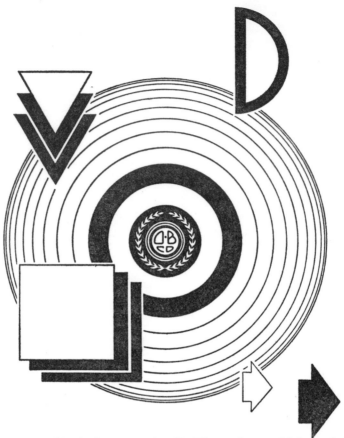

How was this design conceived? The artist couldn't explain—at least, not in words alone. But to the observer (the author), it seemed almost visibly true that the basic process was one of free association.

*   *   *

Isn't it strange, the way a good thing can sometimes lie around for years under our noses, unobserved? That's the story of Free Association. Knowledge of the *principle* of association is as old as psychology itself. But the principle had been utilized almost exclusively in such areas as diagnostic psychology, memory training, educational psychology, personality measurement, and psychotherapy. Only very recently have we begun to appreciate that it can also be utilized for the purpose of creating new ideas—consciously and deliberately.

In your first applications of this new/old technique, you are quite likely to be somewhat handicapped and slowed-down by vague, uneasy feelings about the "practicality" of what you are doing. If so, you may take comfort from the knowledge that virtually every person—virtually every adult person, at least—is similarly inhibited at first by "guilty" feelings about this kind of "day dreaming." You may also take comfort from the knowledge that the remedy is extremely simple: *practice*.

The organized CT technique of Free Association . . .

> the body relaxed,
> the vision inward,
> the mind undiverted,
> a key starting point,
> and a follow-through

. . . is a most practical technique indeed. For it easily meets the most fundamental of all tests of practicality: It works.

Summary

Free Association—A method of stimulating the imagination to some constructive purpose. Procedure:

1. Jot down a symbol—word, sketch, number, picture— which is related in some key way to some important aspect of the problem/subject under consideration.
2. Jot down another symbol suggested by the first one.
3. Continue as in Step 2—*ad lib*—until ideas emerge.

The objective generally is to produce a quantity of intangible ideas, such as advertising slogans, designs, names, etc.

VII. FORCED RELATIONSHIP

Would you like to be a comedian or gag writer, with the ability to turn out new humorous bit after new humorous bit, almost in mass production? According to a humorist friend, this is basically the simplest thing in the world. *Rx:* take the most common situation or trite saying you can imagine; then give this situation/saying an uncommon, opposite-the-usual association;

and it's funny. Roger Price does this with his famous game of "Droodles"—as, for example, by presenting a sketch of what appears to be a circle with a simple grillwork inside, but which he identifies as "a mended doughnut"—thereby "fracturing" his audiences. Thus the principle of *opposites*—that is, the prime base of contrary/unconventional/surprising associations—is a virtually inexhaustible source of humorous invention.

Would you like to be a song writer? You may strive to be another Gershwin or Rodgers or Kern, if you wish (and after any ten minutes of "popular" music, how I hope you will!). But you may begin by being just a *little* creative—that is, by playing musical private-eye, by prying-out and studying the essential styles, meters, themes, etc. of the Three B's and other old masters, then employing *similar* schemes in your own compositions. Is it legitimate, you say? Excuse the tedium: "Everything" at least *"starts* from something else."

Or are you merely trying to entertain a group of youngsters, as on a long, monotonous trip, or a long, rainy day? Then you might play my "Make-a-New-Word" game with them—again utilizing the principle of *opposites*—in the manner of the following transcript:

"Is *Congress* the opposite of *progress?*"

"Only if I get some *appointment* to make up for my *disappointment.*"

"May I end a sentence with a *postposition,* if not a *preposition?*"

"Certainly—because we have *congrams* as well as *programs.*"

"This is no *contest;* it's a *protest.*"

"Well, are you going to *continue* it or *protinue* it?"

"It depends on whether I'm *couraged* or *discouraged.*"

"Let's not *prolong* the agony; let's *conlong* it."

"If *prepaid* is 'paid in advance,' is *postpaid* 'paid in retreat'?"

"I dunno—Boy Scouts are *prepared;* Girl Scouts are *postpared.*"

"Should we *convert* 'em or *provert* 'em?"

"Do you mean as a *preliminary* or as a *postliminary?*"

"Neither—we should get rid of the *backlog* so that we can take care of the *frontlog.*"

These three illustrations, while perhaps elementary and considerably oversimplified here, may give a little helpful insight into some of the nature of our seventh CT technique, the *"Forced Relationship"* technique. This technique is "kissin' kin" to the immediately preceding one, but with at least one very distinctive and important difference: Whereas the object in Free Association is to get the mind to form associations more or less at random, without particular limitation or inhibition, the aim when using the Forced Relationship technique is to get the mind to *focus* in such an oriented, directed way as to *force* relevant associations or relationships into being. Hence the name.

In Forced Relationship, the intent is to compel consideration of *selected* (therefore irrelevance-free) bits of idea-building material; to carry out *controlled* sequences of symbolic activity; in effect, to present the mind with series of information-bits of predetermined type (and to impel it continually to seek-out and present ever more bits of information of like type) and with each presentation to ask of itself, "Any connection? Ring any bells?"

In practical application as an orderly CT method—and in a somewhat more complete and advanced procedure than suggested by our initial illustrations—the Forced Relationship technique is carried out in four steps:

Step 1: Isolate the elements of the problem at hand. Pick out the essential parts and the pertinent facts (and/or "attributes") about the parts. Record this information.

Step 2: Find the relationships between/among these elements —in

... *Similarities.* ("Item A is like Item B.")

... *Differences.* ("C is unlike D.")

... *Analogies.* ("E is to F as G is to H.")

... *Cause and Effect.* ("X occurs because of Y and Z.")

Step 3: Record the relationships.

(Actually, this should be done concurrently with Step 2; but I am listing it separately for the sake of giving it emphasis.)

Step 4: Analyze the record of relationships—to find the patterns (or basic ideas) present. And, from these patterns, *develop new ideas.*

Practice in Point

If you have the procedural pattern pretty well in mind, now, will you please do yourself the favor of clarifying the Forced Relationship technique further by completing the following practice exercise:

In this practice problem, you will deal with three main parts— a yardstick, a ball, and a box. The ball is a perfect sphere (glass) three inches in diameter; hollow, transparent; with walls .015" thick. The box is a paperboard cubicle; four inches (inside) in height, width and depth; open at one end; with walls .030" thick. The yardstick is a common wooden one such as is used as an advertising "give-away."

Now, to get started, take several minutes to perform Step 1; that is, to the information already given, add whatever else you know about the (typical) box, ball and yardstick. (*E.g.: Ball*— rolls, brittle, non-conductor, etc. *Box*—combustible, square-cornered, etc. *Yardstick*—you state it . . .)

Have you *really* recorded everything you can think of about the essential elements of the problem? . . . Better take some more time, and think about it some more.

When you are satisfied that you have gone just about as far as you can with Step 1, go ahead with Steps 2 and 3 ("Find and record the relationships . . ."). Take plenty of time with this, and don't let yourself get over-anxious to start creating ideas; for without this kind of careful preparation you will not be nearly as successful as you can and will be *with* it.

Is your preparation for creation thoroughly done, now? Then let's get to the point of this exercise, which is . . .

Devise new games—as many as you can—*using the ball, box and yardstick*. That is, carry out Step 4: analyze your record of relationships to find the patterns or basic ideas present therein; and, from these, develop your new ideas. If you stick to it for 30 minutes or so, you should be able to think up at least two dozen different games that can be played with the ball, box and yardstick. And—who knows?—maybe one of them will turn out to be the greatest thing since the Hula Hoop . . . and you wouldn't mind *that*, would you?

From your study of the small illustrations provided, and from your experimentation with the game-invention practice exercise, you may have gathered that one of the very special values of the Forced Relationship technique (assuming, of course, that the user applies it thoroughly and properly) is that it *compels* concentrated to-the-point consideration of the very kind of raw material that leads most surely to the building of sound and successful new ideas.

This limited experience and study is hardly adequate, however, to have shown you a certain other, greater value. So won't you please be patient, and take this on faith for a short while?:

The Forced Relationship technique, as delineated here, is perfectly "capable of standing on its own two feet," so to speak. But it is even more potent with, and pivotally important to, still another—and far more comprehensive—method of Creative Thinking. So a little farther along in this book, where I can fit the Forced Relationship technique into a larger, more sophisticated, more valuable context, I will explain it more fully. Promise! For now, then, won't you please just tuck it into your mental "pending file"?

Summary

Forced Relationship—A method which has essentially the same basic purpose as Free Association, but which attempts to *force* associations. Procedures:

1. Isolate the elements of the problem at hand.
2. Find the relationships between/among these elements. (Similarities—Differences—Analogies—Cause and Effect.)
3. Record the relationships in organized fashion.
4. Analyze the record of relationships—to find the patterns (or basic ideas) present. Develop new ideas from these patterns.

VIII. EDISONIAN METHOD

Strictly speaking, our eighth CT technique is not so much a method for formulating new ideas—that is, for conceiving the original hypotheses—as it is an approach to finding ways to make general ideas work *after* they have been formulated.

This approach was used extensively by the famous Thomas Alva Edison and, therefore, has been named the *"Edisonian Method."*

As practiced by Edison and others, *the Edisonian Method consists principally of performing a virtually endless number of trial-and-error experiments.* The experimentation goes on and on and on—for some unknown and unknowable period of time— until the experimenter(s) become successful or, for other reason, cease trying.

For example, in the case of his famous invention, the incandescent electric lamp, Edison began with the general idea of forcing electricity through a fine filament under such "pressure" as to produce light from heat (particle-agitation). But to find a material for making filaments that would stand up under such punishment long enough to be practically usable and commercially feasible, Edison tried *over 1,600* different materials. (The story is probably apocryphal, but it is said that he even tried Limburger cheese.) Small wonder he avowed that invention is "99% perspiration and 1% inspiration"!

"Well, what else *could* Edison have done?" you say. What else, indeed? He was a pioneer working in little-understood wildernesses, with incomplete "maps" and other critical data. And therein, perhaps, is an important tip-off. . . .

In the considered judgment of the scientifically trained CT student, the pure Edisonian Method should invariably be held as a kind of "last ditch" method, to be resorted to only in two clear situations:

> . . . first, when other, more systematic (scientific?) methods have completely failed to produce the desired results; and/ or
>
> . . . second, when one is knowingly and necessarily delving into the unknown, into areas of *basic* search/research.

Illustrative of the first of these situations: Thomas Midgley of General Motors is said to have tried every systematic/scientific approach he could conceive of in his efforts to find a knock-inhibitor for the internal-combustion gasoline engine—and failed. Whereupon he discarded "reasonableness" and started looking for the *un*reasonable. And finally, after trying a fantastic number of compounds, he found one that was "utterly absurd"— tetraethyl lead—but worked. (We can be glad that Midgley and his men didn't stop with the *very* first lead compounds that worked, by the way, for it is said they produced such horrendous, enduring odors that the laboratory workers handling them had to become virtual hermits for a while.)

Illustrative of the fact that the Edisonian Method was *not* Thomas Midgley's habitual first or exclusive CT technique, by the way, while we're about it: In 1930, Midgley undertook to lay the foundation for the development of safe, practicable home refrigerators and air conditioners. This required ignoring the unsatisfactory refrigerants of the day and going to work on the task of finding some substitute that would boil below the freezing point of water and be non-toxic, non-flammable and a few other much-wanted "nons." And Midgley accomplished this very thoroughly and expeditiously—first, by consulting the tables of volatile but stable organic compounds, with their established boiling and melting points; second, by researching the fact that potentially usable fluorine compounds had never been used, probably because of a toxicity factor; third, by deciding to synthesize and test the compound, "dichlorodifluoromethane," which was known to have some of the properties desired; and thereby, finally, producing the completely successful new refrigerant known as Freon.

> Close-call sidelight: Only four small batches of Midgley's new compound could be provided with the raw material available at the time. The first sample, when tested, worked perfectly. But if he had used one of the other three at first, he might have abandoned the whole fluorine-compound idea, because these other three samples were contaminated with a then-unsuspected impurity; and this impurity was toxic, while Freon was not.

A certain, indeterminate amount of Edisonian trial-and-error is no doubt necessary to the development of creative solutions for many problems. And, of course, *every* idea has to be tried sooner or later. But you had better be wary . . .

The limitations and appropriate applications of the Edisonian Method must be kept in mind. Otherwise, it can become a trap —and a trap that will very effectively *block* the paths to new, creative ideas. (A little farther along in the book, where it fits better and more properly into another context, you are going to find out more clearly how and why this is so.) It boils down to this: if you *must* use it, you must—but *only* if you must.

Summary

Edisonian Method—An approach consisting principally of performing a virtually endless number of trial-and-error experiments. A "last-ditch" approach, to be resorted to only . . .

> . . . when other, more systematic methods have completely failed to produce the desired results; and/or
> . . . when one is knowingly and necessarily delving into the unknown, into areas of *basic* search-research.

IX. CHECK-LIST TECHNIQUE

Our ninth CT technique, called the *"Check-List Technique,"* is one that has been in regular use for a long time. In fact, it is quite possible that *you* may already have used it with some regularity, at some time or other, in some field or other, even though at the time of use you might not have thought of it as "a technique of creative thinking."

Essentially, the Check-List Technique consists very simply of *a system for getting idea-clues or "leads" by checking the items on a prepared list against the problem or subject under consideration.*

In many, many different fields of endeavor, there are established, standard check lists which can be used to stimulate the production of ideas. (An immediately preceding short example is the list entitled, "Inhibitors of Creative Thinking," on page 46-47, which can be used as an aid in getting ideas on how to become more creative.) Fundamentally, these lists are of two main types:

1. The problem-delineation ("P-D") list. This kind of list serves, in effect, to put an outline or frame around the problem; to keep CT efforts on the track; to specify the considerations to be dealt with; and thereby to point out *directions* in which pertinent new ideas may lie.

2. *The possible-solution ("P-S") list.* This kind of list serves to provide more direct suggestions as to *how* new ideas may be evolved.

Would you like some "for-instances"? All right; here are two:

"P-D"

If you should be concerned with the making, storing, handling, marketing, selling, distributing, etc. of some consumer product, you might get considerable relevant-new-idea-suggestion aid from this . . .

Package-Planning Check List

I. Product Characteristics
A. Physical form:
    1. Solid?
    2. Liquid?
    3. Gaseous?
    4. Powdered?
    5. Granular?
    6. Fragile solid?
B. Possible hazards:
    1. Mold?
    2. Light?
    3. Vermin?
    4. Bacteria?
    5. Oxidation?
    6. Corrosion?
    7. Pilferage?
    8. Water/vapor?
    9. Infestation?
    10. Color change?
    11. Foreign odors?
    12. Chemical action?

13. Physical damage?
14. Sifting, leakage?
15. Thermal, barometric or humidity changes?
16. Loss of aroma, flavor, volatile contents?

II. *Packaging Material*

A. Appropriateness:
1. Is the material right for the intended use?
2. Does it lend itself readily to the processes of fabrication, graphic arts, etc., giving form and identity?
3. Are related inks, adhesives, etc., suited to the package material and to resistance of the hazards encountered?
4. Is the material familiar to the customer, or will special selling be required?

B. Structural adequacy:
1. Will it endure mechanized, high-speed production?
2. Will it withstand extremes of temperature and refrigeration?
3. Will it stand up under transportation, storing, handling?
4. Will it withstand processes of gas, vacuum or hermetic packing; sterilization, if required?

C. Availability:
1. Is a steady, reliable supply assured?
2. Are delivery dates adequate?
3. Are prices free from fluctuation?
4. Are prices in line with value?
5. Are there multiple sources of supply?

III. *Production Considerations*

A. Equipment:
1. Can the package be formed, filled, measured and closed on existing equipment?
2. Would modifications in the package make it advisable to utilize new equipment?
3. Is provision made for necessary code marking?

B. Personnel:
1. Are special people with special skills required to manufacture the packages?

       2. Does the design lend itself to use of minimum crews?

       3. Are unusual difficulties imposed due to breakage, inspection, etc.?

       4. Are operations mechanized or manual?

       5. Does production involve hazards to the people?

C. Design:

       1. Is the package the right size and shape for moving through machines and conveyors at the required speeds?

       2. Is the closure suitable for the product and for production, as well as for consumer convenience?

       3. Are the openings adapted to filling operations?

       4. Are suitable spaces and surfaces provided for labeling?

       5. Is the design engineered for shock resistance in machine handling?

       6. Is the design proper for storage, shipment and handling?

IV. *Convenience Factors*

A. Prior to use . . .

       1. Are unusual methods or equipment-items required?

       2. Can the component parts of the packages be assembled easily in final packaging?

       3. Can the package be adapted for shipment to the user in end-use cases?

B. Packing/shipping considerations . . .

       1. Is the unit-package suited for bulk packaging and handling?

C. In distribution channels . . .

       1. Is the package of the proper size and shape for convenience of the wholesaler and retailer?

       2. Is the package convenient to store, display, handle, deliver?

       3. Is brand-identification and other related information assured?

       4. Is visibility provided where needed?

D. In the consumer's hands . . .

1. Is the unit packaged of the proper size?
2. Is inspection prior to sale desirable? Possible?
3. Is package opening and re-closing made easy?
4. Are dispensing devices provided? Needed?
5. Can the consumer measure-out desired quantities of contents?
6. Is there a disposal problem? Is provision made for disposal?
7. Is there provision for re-using empty packages, if wanted?
8. Has ease of grasping, dispensing, etc., been provided?
9. Is package-size right for the consumer's storage places?

V. *Considerations of Economy*

A. Does the package use the minimum practicable amount of material?
B. Is the package adaptable to practices making for economy in production, handling, storage, etc.?
C. Is package cost in proper relation to . . .
   1. Unit price of the product?
   2. Available margin?
   3. Market desired?
   4. Class of merchandise packaged?
D. Does the price of the packaging insure a low percentage of defects/rejects?
E. Does the package provide protection for the normal life of the product, plus a safety margin?
F. Is the package economical to ship?
G. Does the "quality" appearance of the package impress the prospective purchaser as desired?

VI. *Merchandising Considerations*

A. The product:
   1. What are its uses?
   2. Is it a new product?
   3. What are its features?
   4. What is its relative quality?
B. The market:
   1. Who are the ultimate consumers?

2. What is the plan of distribution . . .
   a. Mail order?
   b. Supermarkets?
   c. Chain stores?
   d. Direct selling?
   e. Independent stores?
   f. Self-service stores?

C. Buying habits:
1. What are the retailer habits/practices *re* products of this kind in . . .
   a. Unit of purchase?
   b. Storage before sale?
   c. Shelf/counter/window display?
      (1) Single unit attractive?
      (2) Package shape and size suitable?
      (3) Package visible above/below eye-level?
      (4) Which package-panel displayed most prominently?
2. Will the retailer support the product?
3. Will supplementary or point-of-sale support be given?

D. Size considerations:
1. Are package-sizes well suited to . . .
   a. Normal habits of consumers?
   b. Current methods of distribution?
2. How would size-changes affect . . .
   a. Convenience to consumers?
   b. Quantities regularly purchased and used?

E. Competition:
1. How does the product compare with competitive products?
2. How do the respective packages compare in . . .
   a. Materials used?
   b. Sizes, shapes, colors, designs?
   c. Features (both desirable and undesirable)?
3. Should your package resemble competing ones, or should it be different and distinctive—to manufacturer, retailer, consumer?

VII. *Package-Appearance Considerations*

A. Identification factors:
1. Are all essential features present and properly treated?
2. Is the brand name clear and adequately featured?
3. Is the product-maker's name given the right prominence?
4. Can the product be identified on sight?
5. Does or should the product use a "family" design?
6. Does the package, in appearance, reflect . . .
   a. The outstanding qualities of the product?
   b. The manufacturer's integrity/responsibility?
7. Is the package memorable?
8. Is the package "photogenic," as in TV commercials?
B. Informational factors:
1. Does the package carry the information required by law, in a manner acceptable for the distribution planned?
2. Are there special regulations to be observed, such as the cleanliness/sterility of material, etc.?
3. Are directions legible and clear? Price-panel prominent?
4. Do the illustrations serve to inform, interest, attract?
C. Attention-getting factors:
1. Are colors and design . . .
   a. In good taste?
   b. Right in relation to the competition?
   c. Appropriate for the product, outlet, consumer?
2. Does the package make the desired impression . . .
   a. At near-point? At a distance?
   b. In displays? In the home?
   c. Adjacent to other products?
3. Is the package an advertising message in its own right?

VIII. Planning and Coordination Considerations

A. Internally . . .
1. Is there cooperation among . . .
   a. Research and Development?
   b. Marketing?

       c. Purchasing?

       d. Art and Design?

       e. Legal Department?

       f. Production?

       g. Sales and Advertising?

   2. Have conflicts regarding package size, appearance, structure, etc., been resolved?

   3. Have complete specifications for the package been preserved?

B. Externally ...

   1. Have you determined dealer attitudes?

   2. Are you satisfied that consumer acceptance for the product and package can be developed?

It is virtually self-evident, is it not?: If it is your desire to create a new and better packaging program for your product, this "P–D"-type (problem-delineation-type) check list may suggest a myriad of high-potential areas for profitable innovation.

"P–S"

But suppose your problem-at-hand is a matter primarily of improving the methods of performing manual work—as, for example, in typical operations performed at a bench, a desk, an assembly workstation, a kitchen, *ad infinitum*. In this case you might have a great deal to gain from applying a possible-solution- or "P S"-type check list in a three-step procedure, as follows:

Step 1: Make a close, careful, detailed study of the operations performed at the workplace with which you are concerned. Make a sketch of the work-station/area, and observe the related operations until you have a clear picture of the work involved.

Step 2: Check the manual operations performed in your selected work-study against the following list:

Principles of Motion Economy

Check the work against each of these ten principles for clues to changes that may improve the method and reduce fatigue.
- *Keep motion paths of body members within the normal*

working area. (This eliminates unnecessary reaching, stretching, etc., which builds fatigue and reduces speed. The normal work area for the hands is determined by an arc drawn with the sweep of the hands with the fore-arms extended.)

- *Slide small objects, rather than pick them up and carry them.* (Coins, paper clips, washers and similar small objects can be moved to point-of-use much more quickly and easily by sliding than by grasping/carrying.)
- *Avoid sharp changes in direction; plan continuous, curved motion paths.* (This is simply "going along" with natural inertial forces and avoiding the diversion of energy to non-productive uses.)
- *Locate materials and tools in sequence of use.* (Put them where you will use them. This saves back-tracking and waste motion.)
- *Plan repetitive operations for rhythm and automaticity.* (That which can be reduced to automatic habit is thereby made smoother and easier.)
- *Use vises or fixtures for holding material.* (Two hands doing productive work are better than one hand doing productive work while the other is used only for a holding device.)
- *Use drop delivery wherever possible.* (Gravity-power is free power.)
- *Pre-position tools for quick and easy grasp.* (This not only leads to greater speed and ease; it also makes for greater neatness, less get-ready and clean-up work, improved safety, and other values.)
- *Pre-position pieces of material for easy sequence of operations.* (Ditto the "pre-position tools" commentary—plus.)
- *Provide chair of proper height, comfortable seat and back-rest for good posture; provide good illumination, ventilation, noise control and personal treatment.* ('Nuf sed!)

Step 3: Work out and apply the improvements suggested by the ten principles of motion economy.

*   *   *

As you may have discovered already from your study of the sample lists given here, the "plusses" of the Check-List Technique are mainly two-fold:

1. It helps to keep one from overlooking the obvious.
2. It is simple and convenient to use.

The "minuses" of the Check-List Technique, while perhaps not quite so immediately apparent, are similarly double-barreled:

1. A check list is practically never all-inclusive. It does not

cover every aspect of a subject. But the user may be easily lulled into assuming otherwise—and thus find his thinking narrowed to the strict confines of his check list.

2. A check list can become a crutch, a mere substitute for original thinking. And if this happens, of course, it leads the user right back to the inhibitor-pitfalls of mental laziness, superficiality, etc., that he wants and needs so much to avoid.

But just as a mechanical tool, intelligently designed and understandingly applied, extends the power and effectiveness of the human body, so can the Check-List Technique/tool extend the power and effectiveness of the human mind. Plainly, therefore, it will pay you both to search-out present check lists and to develop new check lists pertaining to the fields of your special CT interests.

Summary

Check-List Technique—A system for getting idea-clues or "leads" by checking the items on a prepared list against the problem or subject under consideration. The objective is to obtain a number of general ideas for further follow-up and development into specific form.

X. MORPHOLOGICAL ANALYSIS

In the process of examining the first CT technique on our list (Brainstorming) we found that one of the prime objects of Creative Thinking, regardless of the particular technique(s) employed, is to *think up as many alternative ideas as possible*. Behind this object is the principle that "The greater the quantity of ideas generated, the greater is the likelihood of generating uniquely good ones."

After a person has familiarized himself with a few of the different methods/approaches/techniques of Creative Thinking, and has practiced using them for some time, he often finds that this task of finding "as many alternative ideas as possible" is one that worries him a great deal. He finds himself bothered by nagging thoughts such as: "Am I overlooking something? Have I thought of every possible combination? Are there some angles or slants to this that I don't see? . . ."

One man who was so bothered—and did something constructive about it—is Dr. Fritz Zwicky, world-famous scientist and
professor of astrophysics at the California Institute of Technology. What Dr. Zwicky did specifically about it was develop
what CT students have termed correctly: *"a comprehensive way
to list and examine all of the possible combinations that might
be useful in solving some given problem."* (Note the word *all,*
clearly signifying that this technique provides for the systematic
review of the present-and-familiar *plus* the heretofore-unknown-
but-possible. Quite a promise!) And Dr. Zwicky gave his technique the somewhat formidable title, *"Morphological Analysis."*

Now, contrary to what at least one wag has inferred, the name
of this technique does *not* derive from the words *Morpheus* (god
of sleep) and *logical* (mental), and therefore mean "sleepy-
headed". It derives from the term *morphology,* meaning "the
science of structure or form"—and, as you will see presently, it
has to do with some very wide-awake thinking indeed.

The procedure for applying Morphological Analysis is this:

*Step 1: State your problem as broadly and generally as
possible.* Do *not* state the problem in specific terms as, for
instance, is recommended in the case of the Input-Output
Technique.

*Step 2: Define the independent variables present in the
problem.* Define them as broadly and completely as possible.

*Step 3: Enter the variables as the axes of a morphological
chart.* This will show you—by inspection of the items appear-
ing at the various junctions—"all of the possible combinations
that might be useful" in solving your problem.

*Step 4: Select the most promising alternatives and follow
through*—take your alternatives through testing, verification,
modification, evaluation and development, as required.

"Clear as the usual set of highway directions," you say? I
agree. But read through the four steps several more times, won't
you, to get the general scheme fixed in mind? After that we'll
get to the requisite business of drawing clarifying "maps" and
erecting illuminating "signs".

Review finished? Let's move on, then . . .

Movin' On

Suppose, for the sake of clarifying the use of the four-step procedure for applying the CT technique of Morphological Analysis, that you are an engineer assigned the job of designing a completely new transportation system. Specifically, your detailed assignment calls for a system for transporting a specified number of standard, six-foot, 170-pound people—so many such people per hour—over a particular terrain and distance—at a given rate of speed—under such-and-such climatic conditions—at stated times of day and night—at so-and-so cost per person—*et cetera, so forth, and so on.*

Now, this is such a welter of limiting requirements that it has the almost inevitable effect of hog-tying the imagination. (As my unusually imaginative artist-friend Frank Zimmer so typically reacted, "You'll hear one awful, dull 'thud' out of me if I have to use *that* for a CT springboard!") So, to break free of such enshacklement via the Morphological Analysis method, you might re-state your problem ("Step 1"): *Get people from one place to another by means of a powered vehicle.*

"Step 2: Define the independent variables . . ." then falls into place rather readily:

One independent variable is the *type of vehicle* used—as: *cart, sling, chair, bed.*

A second variable, independent of the first one, is the *media* in which the vehicle operates—as: *air, water, oil, hard surface.*

A third variable, independent of either of the first two, is the *power source*—as: *compressed air, electric motor, steam, magnetic field.*

"Step 3: Enter the variables as the axes . . ." requires the drawing of a morphological chart to fit your particular set of variables. And in this transportation problem, with three independent variables, your chart would take shape as a sort of three-dimensional "cabinet", with each variable—each sub-item thereof, more exactly—"fed" into a separate dimension of the cabinet.

This chart enables you to visualize and scrutinize all of the possible power-media-vehicle combinations in the "drawers" of

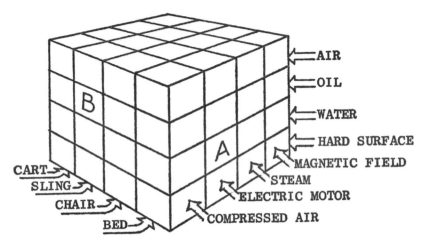

the cabinet. Thus, if you were mentally to open drawer *"A,"* you would find there the possible solution: *a bed driven in water by an electric motor*. Drawer *"B"* would contain *a sling driven through oil by compressed air*. And so on. Altogether, with this particular set of variables (and this set is obviously far from all-

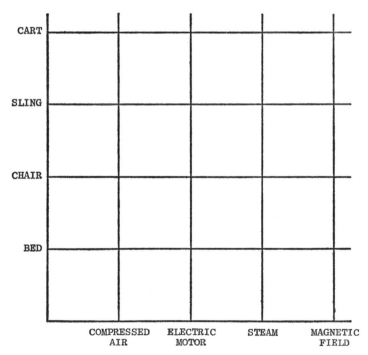

inclusive, as no doubt you are quite aware), you would have *64* possible combinations.

"But what if this problem had only *two* independent variables," you ask? Then you would need to draw only a *double*-axis chart as shown on page 100.

"Why, there are only *16* possible combinations here; and I can easily handle that many in my head, without all this charting," you say? All right. But if you want to make *sure* of considering all 16, and not just 15 . . . And if you make this illustration a little more realistic—say, by adding more power sources such as the gasoline engine, turbine, atomic power plant, gravity, and so on . . . In any event, it's *your* choice.

"Well, what about the problem having *more* than three independent variables, then?" Probably the simplest combination-assembling device is a kind of "permutational listing"—which means nothing more complicated than a vertical-horizontal/cross-comparison listing such as this:

Power	Media	Vehicle	(Variable)
Steam	Air	Bed	. . . .
Compressed Air	Oil	Cart	. . . . . .
Electric Motor	Water	Chair	. . . .
Magnetic Field	Hard Surface	Sling	. . . .

Actually, this variation is much easier than the multi-dimensional charting; and it is equally or more workable, as well. And if you like to "gimmick things up", you can do so very easily with this variation by making up your lists in the form of a simple paper or paperboard slide rule . . .

ollollu cyno	yllo ohon	ollu cynollo	ollollu cyno
ollu cynollo	ollollu cyno	ollu cynollo	ollu cynollo
VARIABLE #1	VARIABLE #2	VARIABLE #3	VARIABLE #4
yllo ohon	ollollu cyno	ollu cynollo	yllo ohon
ollu cynollo	ollu cynollo	yllo ohon	yllo ohon
yllo ohon	yllo ohon	ollollu cyno	ollollu cyno

Then, merely by moving the slides, you can line-up all of the possible combinations and visualize them very rapidly.

*   *   *

What is your particular problem at this moment? One of

decorating—with varying choices in colors, draperies, furniture? One of product-packaging—with alternatives in material and other factors such as we discussed in connection with the Check-List Technique? One of selecting industrial lift trucks—with choices as to type, capacity and fuel? Whatever your problem—whether one like these three or something like none of them—if it revolves around a number of basic variables, the CT technique of Morphological Analysis has pertinence.

It is obvious, of course, that Morphological Analysis does not, in and of itself alone, directly produce a complete, finished end-product. It provides—and attempts only to provide—a mechanical system for listing alternate approaches to solving broadly defined problems. *After* it has done its job, a great deal of imagination, persistence, and hard, detailed work *still* are required to develop any of the alternatives into worthwhile, workable solutions.

The special difficulty in using Morphological Analysis (and this is certainly not exclusive to this technique) is in *isolating the independent variables* in a problem. Sometimes, as no doubt you are already keenly aware, this task alone may require extended, tedious periods of research and study.

When the isolation of the independent variables in a problem is accomplished, however, the special *value* of Morphological Analysis in dealing with the problem from that point forward is that this technique relieves one completely of worry over whether or not some potentially unique and valuable idea has been overlooked. For Morphological Analysis infallibly lives up to its promise—it truly does enable one to "list and examine *all* of the possible combinations that might be useful in solving some given problem."

Summary

Morphological Analysis—A comprehensive way to list and examine all of the possible combinations that might be useful in solving some given problem. Procedure:

1. State your problem as broadly and generally as possible.
2. Define the independent variables present in the problem —as broadly and completely as possible.

3. Enter the variables as the axes of a morphological chart— or make a permutational listing.

4. Select the most promising alternatives and follow them through.

The objective is to find *all* of the possible combinations— for subsequent testing, verification, modification, evaluation and development.

XI. INSPIRED (BIG DREAM) APPROACH

"Boy, how I wish *I* could just dawdle around until I dreamed up sumpin' like the safety pin, and made a fortune!"

"The guy sits out on a beach or a mountain top or somewhere, see; and he stares off in the distance . . . Then, after a while, he gets his painting outfit and smears around on a canvas—and makes *thousands* for the picture. Some guys have all the luck!"

"If only *I* could pick ideas out of thin air, like writers and cartoonists and such, I'd have it made. But look at me—man, I gotta *work* for a living!"

"Did you hear about the fellow who got woke up in the middle of the night by a voice that told him how to invent a carburetor for goin' a hunnert miles to the gallon? Yeah, some oil company bought him out, they tell me . . ."

"Those composers just hang around a piano, and diddle and fool till they get an inspiration . . . How easy can you have it?"

"The way I get it, the company has these here big-domes, see; and they sit up in some tower, somewheres, with their feet on the desks, lookin' off on cloud nine; and they just kinda make their minds blank—doze-like, you know—till these crazy schemes come to 'em . . ."

Do these excerpts from *vox populi* sound familiar? Small wonder—for they are exact quotations. And there is good reason to believe that these comments are a representative cross-section, a revealingly typical sample of what, in some vague way, passes through the mind of many and many a person in direct association with the term "creative thinking."

Which is one way, at least, of saying that (as usual?) the popular conception is *almost* correct—for there is, indeed, an "inspiration-type" CT technique. And this technique is known as the *"Inspired (or 'Big Dream') Approach."*

Where those unacquainted with the organized body of CT knowledge get badly misled, in giving only cursory thought to this technique, however, is in assuming that it consists merely of sitting quiescently on one's big, fat nether-end—*doing nothing, that is*—until some mysterious genie, leprechaun or Divine Providence sends him his very own, richly deserved bolt from the blue. And, in the vernacular, that jest plain ain't so. In *any* idiom, it *still* ain't so!

As practiced by consistently successful creative producers, the so-called Inspired Approach is applied as a deliberate, definite, thorough-going, three-phase procedure:

Phase 1: Think the biggest dream possible—about something to benefit mankind. Think to yourself: "What is the most wonderful thing that I might cause to happen to/for people? What is it that people most want and need? If I could create *anything,* what would I choose to create?" And pin-down the *one* thing among your responses that will hold your intent interest, not just momentarily, but over a sustained period.

Phase 2: Read, study and think about every subject connected with your big dream—and do so regularly, persistently and continually.

Phase 3: Drop down a dream or so—then engineer your dream into reality. When in due course you perceive that at least *part* of your big dream can be realized and brought to fruition—even though imperfectly—go to work on the task of bringing it to this practical reality. (If one aspires to be a "beautiful dreamer" but fails to perform this third and vital "do" operation, he accomplishes nothing of consequence. He may think up new ideas—vague, ill-defined ones, for the most part—but he will find that someone else has been thinking them up, too . . . and then some.)

Case histories of successful innovators show that sometimes this process/procedure called Inspired Approach results in spectacular advancements. The histories also show that these advancements came from performing *all* of the three, key, Big-Dream functions.

One of the most notable modern Inspired Approach cases is

that of the *Polaroid Land Camera,* created by Dr. Edwin Land, president and research director of the Polaroid Company. In studying this case, it is easy to observe that Dr. Land started by "thinking the biggest dream possible"; imagining—he being something of a "shutter bug"—that the world wanted and needed instantaneous, full-color photographs. But what superficial investigation fails to disclose is that Land had to cut back his dream from full color to "sepia tone"; and he also had to work out the mechanics, the chemistry, the optics—even the basic concepts of film manufacture—before his dream was of any use.

True: Edwin Land's Big Dream was the beginning of his remarkable camera. But his Big Work brought it to reality.

In another famous case, King Gillette dreamed of finding something that the general public would use briefly, discard when used, and buy again and again. (This is still just about as smart a formula as anyone has yet devised for making good: Invent something which "costs a dime, sells for a dollar, and is habit-forming.") According to his own testimony, the fundamental idea for Gillette's safety razor with disposable blade occurred to him "in a flash" one morning in 1895. But he did not secure a patent until 1904. And it took him and his inventor-partner William Nickerson six years to work out satisfactory methods of producing inexpensive blades from sheet steel. So again: a Big Dream—*plus* the vital Big Work . . .

And perhaps this is something which is basic to *all* significant, enduring, creative endeavor, regardless of related methodology:

> A deep desire to produce something of benefit to mankind, plus
>
> A constancy in the pursuit of relevant knowledge, plus
>
> An abiding willingness to engage in pertinent hard work, plus
>
> Acceptance of the probable inevitability of the conclusion by the uninitiate: "If *I* had a nice workplace, and a secretary, and all that, I'll betcha *I* could dream up new stuff, too!"

C'est la vie!

C'est la Reverie Magnifique!

Summary

Inspired (Big Dream) Approach—A "breakthrough" approach which sometimes leads to spectacular advancements. Procedure:

1. Think the biggest dream possible about something to benefit mankind.
2. Read, study and think about every subject connected with your "big dream"—and do so regularly, persistently, continually.
3. Drop down a dream or so, then engineer your dream into reality.

The objective is to make the greatest possible achievement for human benefit.

PRACTICAL PRACTICE

If you are studying this book with the sincere and serious intention of increasing your idea-productivity (why else?) I believe that, at this point, just about the smartest thing you can do is this:

1. *Delineate your particular areas of interest.* To aid you in this, here is a list from which you may wish to choose areas, or which may suggest the areas, in which you are most interested in applying your creative abilities:

Advertising	Energy	Humor	Medicine
Air	Engineering	Illustration	Men
Apparel	Entertainment	Implements	Methods
Automation	Erosion	Industry	Mining
Aviation	Farming	Instruments	Motivation
Building	Fashion	Inventory	Music
Business	Firefighting	Jewelry	Names
Carpentry	Food	Journalism	Navigation
Chemistry	Friction	Keys & Locks	News
City Planning	Fuels	Kitchens	Novelties
Color	Furniture	Landscaping	Oil
Communication	Games	Light	Offices
Cooking	Gardening	Locomotion	Organs
Cost Control	Government	Mail	Paper
Decoration	Hats	Management	Personnel
Design	Health	Manufacturing	Pharmacy
Diet	Heat	Marketing	Photography
Diplomacy	Homes	Materials	Physics
Electricity	Human Relations	Mechanics	Planning

Peace	Safety	Upholstery	Words
Pneumatics	Sanitation	Usage	Writing
Policies	Selling	Utensils	Xenons
Printing	Sound	Utilities	Xericity
Products	Steam	Vacations	Xylography
Productivity	Stenography	Vegetation	Yachting
Programming	Storage	Ventilation	Yarn
Psychology	Surgery	Vigilance	Yeast
Public Relations	Tailoring	Vigor	Yield
Purchasing	Teaching	Vocations	Youth
Quality	Time	Vulcanizing	Zeal
Quantity	Tools	Warning	Zest
Quiet	Toys	Waste	Zinc
Recording	Transportation	Weather	Zippers
Refrigeration	Umbrage	Weight	Zoning
Retailing	Unity	Welfare	Zymes

2. *List each of your interest-areas with each of its related, specific sub-problems, items or subjects.* For example, if a selected general area of interest is "Aviation", list this; then add the related particulars—which might be such airplane-items as "yaw reduction", "boundary-layer control", "instrumentation", "airfoil design", "integrated control systems", "structural simplification", "navigational methods/equipment", "weight reduction", "VTOL mechanisms", and so on.

3. *Review the summary of techniques entitled, "Eleven Creative Thinking Techniques," on the following pages.* Think deeply and at length about these techniques in connection with the problems/items you listed in "Step 2", immediately preceding.

4. *Match-up your problems with appropriate techniques*—as provided for on page 108. Decide which of the techniques is likely to be best suited for aiding in the generation of creative solutions for each of your problems.

5. *Go to work: apply the selected techniques to the selected problems.*

ELEVEN CREATIVE THINKING TECHNIQUES

Brainstorming: An intentionally uninhibited, conference type, group approach. Four "ground rules" are observed:

1. Judicial thinking must be withheld—until ideation is carried out.

2. "Free wheeling" is welcomed.
3. Quantity (of ideas) is wanted.
4. Combination and improvement (of ideas) are sought.

The objective is to produce the greatest possible number of alternative ideas for later evaluation and development.

Gordon Technique: A variation of brainstorming with these main features:

1. The chairman leads a general group discussion of a subject which is central to the problem to be solved.
2. The chairman does not reveal the specific problem-assignment to the group until he feels that the group is getting close to a satisfactory solution.
3. The group has a free discussion, with the chairman only questioning and guiding and occasionally supplying problem-related information.
4. When the group seems close to a good solution(s), the chairman reveals the specific problem—whereupon the principle behind the solution is crystallized, and the group then develops the idea in detail.

The objective usually is to produce *one* best idea and to carry it through to testing, verification, development, and production in final form.

Attribute Listing: A technique used principally for improving tangible things. Procedure:

1. Choose some object to improve.
2. List the parts of the object.
3. List the essential, basic qualities, features or attributes of the object and its parts.
4. Systematically change or modify the attributes.

The objective is to better-satisfy the original purpose of the object, or to fulfill a new need with it.

Input-Output Technique: A method for solving dynamic-system design problems. Procedure:

1. Specify the input—the power or force going into the system.

2. Specify the output—the corresponding action/reaction sought.
3. Define the limiting requirements or specifications.
4. Bridge the gap between input and output—find ways to make the input produce the desired output within the specified limitations.

The objective is to produce a number of possible solutions which can then be tested, evaluated and developed.

Catalog Technique: Simply the reference to various and sundry catalogs as a means of getting ideas that will, in turn, suggest other ideas.

Free Association: A method of stimulating the imagination to some constructive purpose. Procedure:

1. Jot down a symbol—word, sketch, number, picture—which is related in some key way to some important aspect of the problem or subject under consideration.
2. Jot down another symbol suggested by the first one.
3. Continue as in Step 2—*ad lib*—until ideas emerge.

The objective generally is to produce a quantity of intangible ideas, such as advertising slogans, designs, names, and so on.

Forced Relationship: A method which has essentially the same basic purpose as Free Association, but which attempts to force associations. Procedure:

1. Isolate the elements of the problem at hand.
2. Find the relationships between/among these elements. (Similarities—Differences—Analogies—Cause and Effect)
3. Record the relationships in organized fashion.
4. Analyze the record of relationships—to find the patterns (or basic ideas) present. Develop new ideas from these patterns.

Edisonian Method: An approach consisting principally of performing a virtually endless number of trial-and-error experiments. A "last-ditch" approach, to be resorted to only

. . . when other, more systematic methods have completely failed to produce the desired results; and/or

. . . when one is knowingly and necessarily delving into the unknown, into areas of basic research.

Check-List Technique: A system for getting idea-clues or "leads" by checking the items on a prepared list against the problem or subject under consideration. The objective is to obtain a number of general ideas for further follow-up and development into specific form.

Morphological Analysis: A comprehensive way to list and examine all of the possible combinations that might be useful in solving some given problem. Procedure:

1. State your problem as broadly and generally as possible.
2. Define the independent variables present in the problem— as broadly and completely as possible.
3. Enter the variables as the axes of a morphological chart— or make a permutational listing.
4. Select the most promising alternatives and follow them through.

The objective is to find *all* of the possible combinations—for subsequent testing, verification, modification, evaluation and development.

Inspired (Big Dream) Approach: A "breakthrough" approach which sometimes leads to spectacular advancements. Procedure:

1. Think the biggest dream possible—about something to benefit mankind.
2. Read, study and think about every subject connected with your big dream—and do so regularly, persistently, continually.
3. Drop down a dream or so, then engineer your dream into reality.

The objective is to make the greatest possible achievement for human benefit.

Technique	*Applications*
Brainstorming	_____
	_____

Gordon Technique ....   ————————————————

                            ————————————————

Attribute Listing ....   ————————————————

                            ————————————————

Input-Output Technique   ————————————————

                            ————————————————

Catalog Technique ....   ————————————————

                            ————————————————

Free Association ....   ————————————————

                            ————————————————

Forced Relationship ......   ————————————————

                            ————————————————

Edisonian Method ....   ————————————————

                            ————————————————

Check-List Technique ..   ————————————————

                            ————————————————

Morphological Analysis   ————————————————

                            ————————————————

Inspired Approach ....   ————————————————

                            ————————————————

Sixth

IS THERE A 'SPECIAL' METHOD?

Yes, of course, you're right—I promised to explore *twelve* techniques of Creative Thinking with you, but so far have delved into only eleven. In a moment I'll get to the twelfth one. First, though, some important preliminaries . . .

In my presentation of CT techniques up to this point, as no doubt you are quite aware, I have tried to move along at a fairly brisk pace, endeavoring to cover the essentials and the fundamental features of each technique, but refraining from making highly detailed explanations. And there were (and still are) three main reasons for this:

1. *Each of the eleven techniques is basically simple and easy to understand.* And understanding can be extended readily through supplementary reading and other means; about which, more later.
2. *Once the principles underlying these eleven techniques are understood, mastery of the techniques becomes mostly a matter of practice.* And each one of us can practice effectively on his own, without need of special assistance.
3. *Frankly, I was building toward the twelfth technique—* which, as you will see presently, will be gone into in some depth and detail.

And why, you may wonder, is this twelfth method of Creative Thinking so climactic, so set apart for extra emphasis, so in need of special treatment? Here's why:

Each of the foregoing eleven techniques is somewhat specialized. Thus, each is limited in that it is most applicable to selected problems or situations. Granted, this also provides certain advantages in that it makes for versatility, resourcefulness, adaptability. But there is more . . .

Both individually and in the aggregate, these eleven techniques have some serious shortcomings—certain deficiencies, undesirable features, overlookings-of-vital-operations, inadequacies, failures-to-take-into-account. Thus, they are incomplete.

We have need of a single, complete, universally applicable method—for ease, economy, convenience and, most of all, for efficiency and efficacy. And this, I believe, is what you will find that you *will* have in the twelfth technique of Creative Thinking.

Bon Appetit

Does this whet your appetite? I hope so. But hold on for a moment. Before you start satisfying your hunger, here are six things you should know:

First, the name: I have named this twelfth CT method the *PackCorp Scientific Approach*—hereinafter, *"PakSA"*—in honor of the Packaging Corporation of America, whose men of management have been more steadfastly appreciative of, and receptive to, new ideas than any other business/industrial group with whom I have ever been personally associated.

Second: This method/technique/approach is *not* "scientific" in the sense of being a "precision method", or in the purposely loose, vaguely suggestive connotation ("automatic . . .", *etc., ad infinitum, ad nauseam*) so dear to some advertising copy writers. Rather, it is scientific in the sense of being *orderly, systematic, organized, thorough.*

Third: The *PakSA* should not be thought of as entirely replacing the other CT techniques. Instead, it should be regarded as a kind of modified combination and extension of the others in which there is an endeavor to accomplish three worthwhile gains:

> *Include and utilize the best features of the other techniques.*
> *Reduce or eliminate the others' limitations and disadvantages.*
> *Add certain special strengths of its own.*

Fourth: This method is relatively simple, but it is no snap.

It contains no "gimmicks" for getting out of all effort. It is, however, an effective formula for working *efficiently* toward the desirable goal of creating "new ideas which will satisfy some expressed or implied need of mankind".

Fifth: In the most literal sense, the *PakSA* was not "developed" at all—*it developed itself.* More specifically, it grew out of the long-standing, continuing habit of observing/analyzing/studying the largely unconscious *natural* methods and mental processes of highly creative men and women.

> To my knowledge, very few of these people ever tried to isolate a CT formula, or even to become conscious of following any particular plan of thinking. Rather, they have been occupied with the creating itself, not the determining of the "how" of it; they have been interested in the action, not its explanation. But their work indicates clearly that they did tend to rely upon certain definite procedures; and analysis shows further that this PackCorp Scientific Approach, albeit modified, refined and extended here, basically has been the most common and productive one—even though its users seemingly have been remarkably unaware of "knowing" the formula.

Thus, while I would be proud indeed to have created this method originally, the truth is that it was *concluded* out of the successful experience of people far more creative than I. And I have only deduced the method, extended it, articulated it, tested it—and found it good.

Finally: The PackCorp Scientific Approach—or *PakSA*—is an integrated system that works better, and more consistently so, than any other single method I know. And here, now, is *how* it works . . .

I. PICK A PROBLEM

If you want to begin PakSA-CT correctly the *first* time, without a lot of false starts or futile "wheel-spinning," begin by forgetting all about "ideas" and "thinking" as such. Exercise the very greatest of control and concentrate instead and exclusively on quite a different task—the task of *finding something to think up ideas about.*

Do you think I am being unnecessarily emphatic, or academic, or "dramatic"—or too formal or systematized—or, perhaps, even dilatory or heel-dragging? Not a bit of it!

A great many well-motivated people never even "get off the ground" in CT because they merely look around aimlessly, randomly, hoping somehow to *stumble* upon ideas. Or they sit passively, fuzzily feeling that "inspiration" is just *bound* to set in eventually (like senility?). Or they merely wait-around, with some sort of vague, wistful notion about "keeping the mind open" for ideas.

The result of this "beginning"—which is really an ending—is that these people fritter away their time and simply bog down eventually in a quagmire of futility, and thus create not new ideas but new *barriers* to creativity. Why? Because the human mind doesn't even *work,* let alone work effectually, that way.

The mind can not consistently create new ideas just by being made *available* to receive them. Neither can it regularly make worthwhile creations out of miscellaneous flotsam that drifts in accidentally through holes in the head. Nor can it create merely upon being exhorted or commanded to do so. And merely keeping the mind "open," like an oyster lying torpidly in the mud, accomplishes nothing creative.

As the famous G. K. Chesterton once said, "The object of opening the mind, as of opening the mouth, is to shut it again on something solid."

The "something solid" needed for CT is something that will *stimulate* the mind, make it go to work. The mind must *ACT* in the Art of Creative Thinking. For creation is dynamic, not static. And the solid-something that supplies both the spark or catalyst to start the creative process, and the fuel to sustain it, is, very simply—a problem.

Now, this may not be the most glamorous beginning imaginable, but let us make no mistake about it—*it is the only beginning that really works!*

C. F. Kettering, the genius of General Motors and one of the most creative men of our time, put it clearly when he said, "All research is simply finding out what's wrong with a thing, then fixing it."

Do you remember the two little one-minute exercises—page 5

—where you first tried to think up new ideas in a vacuum, so to speak, with no starting point; and then you tried to think up ideas concerning an automobile-fault (problem) that bothered you? Do you also remember the difference in *results,* one beginning vs. the other?

So—*pick a problem.*

This sounds so simple and easy, doesn't it? "Just pick a problem. Why, anybody can easily 'pick a problem' because everybody has 'em." At least, that is the surface appearance. But look out! As is the case with so many such appearances, when we dig beneath the top layer of this one, we find that just the *opposite* is true.

The plain truth, as verified by every highly creative person and every experienced CT student I know, is this: *Choosing a problem and stating it properly is one of the most difficult and pivotal operations in the entire creative process!*

The importance (and difficulty) lies not so much in the choosing of a problem as in the *stating* of it, because the statement of the problem is the base from which all subsequent thinking springs. It therefore shapes, colors and directs this thinking. More: the statement of a problem determines—no, *pre*determines —the very scope, range and depth of thought that will ensue.

Stating a problem poorly is the surest way I know to lead oneself at the outset into confused mazes, blind alleys, wasted effort and general futility. Conversely, stating a problem well is the surest way I know to orient and organize oneself (and others in a CT group) for an effective attack on the problem.

John Dewey, described by many as America's most profound philosopher, was so right when he said, "A problem well stated is half solved."

The importance of this requisite first step can hardly be overemphasized. For it is, literally, *sine qua non.*

Two Key Operations

Now, in the foregoing, I have given *Step 1—Pick a Problem* in such a way as to permit the ready assumption that this is a single operation. In actual performance, however, it consists of *two* key operations:

A: Define the Problem

First: Define the problem. Further, define it in writing. Moreover, put your definition into a particular form—*always,* if it is at all possible, *express it as a declarative statement of "what is wrong"*; what is unsatisfactory; what needs fixing; the "lowest common denominator"; the fundamental cause(s) or difficulty(ies); the specific, essential, basic fault or faults.

Our usual impulse, of course, is to state a problem as a broad, general question. ("How can we increase productivity?") And why not? Here's why not:

If the problem is stated as a question, our conditioned impulse is to start an *immediate,* random, urgent (frenzied?) search for *answers.* (Heaven help us, we have even made national heroes of TV-question answerers!) And this forces us directly—even involuntarily—into superficial thinking, into solutions-too-soon-arrived-at. It makes us resort at once and practically exclusively to *memory,* not our creative abilities. And it causes us to be diverted from, and to bypass or disregard, the very operations that lead most surely to satisfactory new solutions.

But when we express the problem as a statement—a statement of "something wrong"—our natural response is to think, *"How come?"* And this promptly puts us on the right track for Creative Thinking.

For example, if your most important problems should happen to be those of a typical executive in a manufacturing enterprise, then . . .

What Needs Fixing—Problems with MACHINES?

DON'T say this:	*Say THIS:*
How can we increase machine output?	Too many set-ups and adjustments are required.
	Work piles up, holds up succeeding operations.
	Machines are complicated and "temperamental".
	Equipment is dirty, dingy, hard to operate.
	Breakdowns are frequent, etc.

What Needs Fixing—Problems with MATERIALS?

DON'T say this:
How can we cut out
material costs?

Say THIS:
Workers wait for stock, supplies,
   materials.
Delivery of incoming materials is slow.
Expensive materials are thrown away.
Waste, spoilage and scrap are high.
Quality is substandard, etc.

What Needs Fixing—Problems with METHODS?

DON'T say this:
How can we raise
our efficiency?

Say THIS:
Jobs are complicated and difficult to
   perform.
A great deal of trimming/finishing is
   done.
Workers have to do a lot of walking,
   lifting, stooping, reaching, etc., in
   their jobs.
Material-handling is clumsy and awk-
   ward.
Workplaces are untidy and disarranged.
Tools are scattered and hard to find.
Bottlenecks hold up production.
Operator fatigue is high, etc.

What Needs Fixing—Problems with MEN?

DON'T say this:
How can we improve
our people's
performance?

Say THIS:
It takes too long to break-in people on
   jobs.
People aren't interested in their work,
   and make a lot of careless mistakes.
There is lack of cooperation and team-
   work.
There are complaints about the pay
   system.
The people are irritable and grouchy.
Absenteeism is high, etc.

What Needs Fixing—Problems with MERCHANDISING?

DON'T say this:	*Say THIS:*
How can we increase our sales?	Our customers are turning to other products.
	Salespeople don't know their jobs.
	Our advertising is ineffective.
	Customer-service is poor, etc.

B: Define Your Objective

Second: Define your objective. (Is it necessary to add "in writing"?)

This means: State your *desired accomplishment*—your *aim or goal*—the *end-result wanted*—the *rationale* (the reason for taking any action on the problem at all)—*the situation or set of conditions to be established or obtained as a consequence of your CT efforts—that which you want to exist when you have created what you set out to create.*

This is the operation in which one very effectively delineates the scope and depth and magnitude of the problem, and determines the quality and nature of the thinking to be invested in it.

And this is the operation wherein *direction* of creative thought is established, so that this thought is kept "homed-in on target."

If these are not reasons enough for giving great care to defining your objective, here is another: The end-objective, however stated, provides the *only* rational basis for making sound, subsequent *evaluation* of the ideas that are ultimately obtained.

These three points are tremendously important to successful CT; so even at the risk of some tedium, please let's re-state them: In defining your CT-problem objective, you . . .

Settle upon the dimensions of the problem. (At least, you decide its size as far as *you* are concerned.) Thus you predetermine the very character and quality—the very depth and imaginativeness—of the thinking that you will bring to bear upon the problem.

Fix in advance your starting point and destination—your

terminals—thus fixing the requisite points for plotting a true, direct course to your goal.

Establish your criteria—set the standards which will enable you to determine, when you have finished your CT effort, whether or not you have achieved what you wanted to achieve.

> This is probably as good a place as any to point out that these already-difficult operations are made even more complicated and difficult by words, terms or "labels", because these tools of expression not only carry along with them a clutter of inhibiting conceptual and emotional associations, but they are inexact and frequently carry misleading meanings. For example, what do these "simple" words mean?:

> Fix _____
> Pipe _____
> Light _____
> Make it fast _____

> Perhaps the thought occurs to you that this difficulty could be eliminated through the use of more exact, precise symbols, such as numbers. Perhaps so; but even the language of "math" can be confused and confusing. For example . . .
> $3 \times 5 - 2 \times 4 = ?$
> Personally, I get four different answers for this problem, and I'm none too sure which, if any, is correct. How about you?

It is no simple, easy thing to formulate precise definitions of CT problems and objectives. But it is critically important that it be done—and done well. Everything that follows rests upon it.

For Example

To see more clearly how important the definition of problem and objective can be, let's examine some cases . . .

In an industrial Creative Thinking Workshop in which I was an observer, here (condensed) is what the group first produced:

Problem (given by Supervisor/Chairman): How can we get more storage space for our department? (Note: a question, not a statement.)

Objective: Get more storage space.

Ideas: Convince management that we need more storage space (and sundry variations on this same theme).

Management said, "No, you can't have more space. You'll have to figure out something else." Whereupon the group went back to work, reluctantly, but with this result:

Problem: Ten different kinds of raw material are stored at random in this production area. Some of them are handled and rehandled five or six times before being put into production. Passageways are blocked by stored materials. 90% of the orders call for only three different kinds of material. Handling damage results in the waste/destruction of 25% of the material in storage. Policy (established five years ago) requires keeping an inventory of materials in departmental storage sufficient for 10 days' production. Production is slow. It requires an average of 30 minutes just to obtain a particular material from storage, let alone get it onto a machine and complete the make-ready for running. High humidity in this production area causes deterioration of stored raw materials to the extent of about 5% loss of material per month of storage. Certain lots of material (three types, valued at more than $3,000) have been stored in the department for more than two years, during which time they have deteriorated to the point where they will have to be thrown out ("when we can find time to get them from the bottom of the pile, which is 30 feet high"). The men are discouraged . . .

Need we go any further? Is this not an altogether different problem—or set of problems—than first "defined" by the group?

For the practice, why not see what definition of *objective* you would make for this problem; then list your ideas for attaining that objective? I'll bet my bottom buck that you'll come up with something a whale of a lot more original than this group first did!

* * *

A number of years ago, with great anticipation, I "signed up" for and attended a university-level Creativity Seminar which was launched enthusiastically with a "Group Think-Up" (really, in essence, a king-size brainstorming session) which went like this:

Problem: How can we improve the automobile windshield wiper? (Again note—a question, not a statement.)

Objective: _____?_____ (None was ever stated.)

Ideas: Use a plastic blade . . .

Longer arms . . .

Wipe back and forth, not in arcs . . .

Wipe up and down . . .

    . . . and so on, hackneyedly, dully, unoriginally.

In about 15 minutes, this session ground to a complete, dead halt. Glancing sidewise at the various participants (who were doing the same) it was easy to see that they felt foolish, ashamed and frustrated.

After a few moments of embarrassed silence, with no one knowing quite what to do, one man finally jumped up and blurted, "What in _____ is the problem? *Why* are we supposed to improve the windshield wiper? What's *wrong* with it? The one on *my* car works all right."

Bless this fellow (who deserves better than anonymity, but whom I never did get to meet, unfortunately); he got this group finally to redesign its whole approach to the problem, like this:

    Problem: Moisture and foreign matter destroy the transparency, parallelism and optical flatness of the windshield.

    Objective: (Again, none was stated. This time, however, it is pretty nearly self-evident, is it not?)

    Ideas: Use the principle of the electric Precipitron (TM) to repel/precipitate dirt particles.

        Blow streams/jets of air across the windshield.

        Build up the windshield with thin, laminated plastic sheets; when the outer one gets dirty, peel it off and throw it away.

        Construct a push-button, extendable "porch roof" that will move forward and protect the windshield from snow and rain.

        Use a chemical that will break down the surface tension of the rain water, thus "smoothing" it.

        . . . and so on and on and on.

"But," you say, "in this second approach, the *wiper* was completely ignored." Exactly! The group concentrated upon exploring the zillion *other* ways to skin the windshield cat, thereby increasing astronomically their chances of coming up with unusual, one-in-a-million ideas.

"Yes, but exactly how *practical* are the ideas in this second batch," you ask? At the moment, who cares? The point is that the first statement of the problem did not lead to original thinking, while the second statement did. Maybe *all* of the second-batch ideas are impractical; but you can't determine the practicality of new ideas if you never get any.

"One last question," you say. "If I'm in the business of manufacturing windshield wipers, do you think for one moment that I'm going to junk my entire investment to take a flyer on some revolutionary device?"

I don't know. All I can say is that I'm glad I'm not in that spot. Because, if I were, I'm afraid I would be lying awake nights, worrying over what would happen to my investment if a keen competitor should come up with some smart new ideas before I did.

*   *   *

Let's examine just one more for-instance, the central figures of which are a machine and its product . . .

Here's how many people would likely deal with it:

Problem: The common *electric toaster* is unattractive, toasts unevenly, is hard to clean, has limited capacity, is bulky and cumbersome to handle and store, has a troublesome cord, is potentially dangerous . . . (Say! Why should *I* do all the work here? *You* have a toaster, so *you* define the problem:)

_____

_____

Objective: Improve the toaster.
Ideas: Paint it rather than chrome-plate it . . .
        Shorten and coil the cord . . .
        Put in a crumb-catcher . . .
        (Continue:) _____

_____

_____

_____

_____

_____

_____

_____

_____

_____

_____

Now, here's how others might deal with the same problem:

Problem: (Probably much the same as in the previous statement.)

Objective: (*Product*-centered, rather than machine-centered:) Develop a new method for converting the starches in various bakery products (bread and other items of various shapes, sizes and types) into glucose—a method for making the products attractive in appearance (golden brown in color), warm at the time of consumption (85 to 100 degrees F.?), tasty, crisp . . . (You take it from here, and spell-out what *you* would like to have:)

_____

_____

Ideas: Use ultrasonics . . .

Employ the radio-wave, electronic-cooking principle . . .

Package pieces individually; treat them chemically so that, when the package is opened to the air, chemical action will produce the result desired. Develop new recipes or formulas, i.e., for *pre*-conditioning the products at the bakery.

(Keep 'em coming:) _____

_____

_____

_____

_____

_____

_____

There is a great deal of difference between these two approaches and in the results obtained, one vs. the other. Do you wonder which is the right one? I can't say. Only you can tell. Because it isn't a question of "right" or "wrong." It is a question of: What is your *objective*—what do you want to *accomplish?*

The manner in which one defines a problem profoundly influences the manner in which he thinks about the problem.

Summary

Step 1: Pick a Problem.
Define the problem—in writing.
First, state what's wrong—what needs fixing.
Second, state your objective—what end-result you seek.

II. GATHER RAW MATERIAL

From time to time, as you have read previous parts of this book, you have been asked to carry out a number of practice exercises, answer "quizzes", solve illustrative problems, and the like. Correct? And these have helped you by providing clarification and illumination of key points, interest-enhancement, personal insight, and other values. Right?

It will come as no surprise to you, then, that I am going to ask you in a moment to carry out still another exercise-in-point. (Besides, Step 1 of PakSA *is* "Pick a problem," no?) So . . .

There is a new and special requirement to be observed in connection with this problem-exercise, however; and that is: Do not read beyond this particular paragraph and attempt to carry out the exercise entirely by yourself. Rather, enlist the help of another person—hereinafter to be known as your "Problem Administrator"—hand the book to this person, with the book open at this page; ask him to read and follow the directions below; then proceed as directed.

*   *   *

Directions to Problem Administrator: It is important to the successful completion of this exercise that it be carried out under carefully controlled conditions. Please, therefore . . .

1. Do not let your reader-friend see what you do in performing "2", below.
2. Turn to page 127. Cut out the four quadrilateral "shapes" outlined there, taking care to do an accurate job. (A razor blade, a straight edge and, by all means, a protective paperboard backing sheet, should serve quite well.) Put the pieces together in random arrangement, and keep them in hand.
3. Read the following, aloud, to your reader-friend:

    In a moment, I am going to hand you four pieces of paper. Originally, these were a single, square piece; but I cut the square into these four pieces.
    That is "the problem"—or "what is wrong".
    The "objective" is to re-assemble the four pieces on a flat plane so as to form a solid, perfect square. Further, you are to accomplish this within exactly two minutes. At the end of this time, whether you have accomplished the objective or not, you must stop and return the four pieces to me.

Cut out the four pieces outlined below, obtaining four congruent pieces.

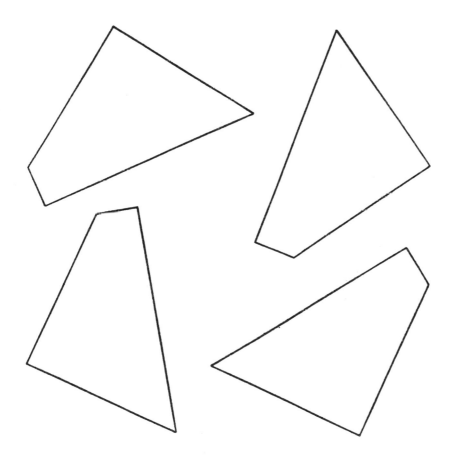

4. Hand the four pieces to your reader-friend, and follow through as per "3". When you repossess the pieces, insert them into the book at page 139, and instruct the reader to continue his reading of the text. Hand the book back to him so that this can be done.

Many thanks for your help!

*   *   *

Now, then . . . What happened?

No, I don't mean: "Did you solve the problem?" Frankly, I don't give a hoot whether you solved it or not—and neither should you! For except as it might involve your pride (which *neither* of us has any wish to hurt, believe me), that is of little importance at the moment.

I mean this: What did you *do* in trying to solve the problem? What *methods* did you employ? After "Step 1" (wherein, in this instance, you were presented with, rather than "picked", a problem), what *step* did you take next? What *procedure* did you follow?

Most people, in attempting to cope with this four-part-square problem—especially under the controlled, "pressurized" conditions imposed—start an immediate, over-anxious, scrambling, shuffling-around of parts. ('Fess up, now—you, too?) In other words, they resort to the Edisonian, or trial-and-error, method. And why not?

This square problem has so few parts or elements that it seems as though it would be easy to solve simply by trying all of the possible arrangements until the right one is found. But a little simple arithmetic, applied to the problem, will show how inappropriate this method is.

Relative to any starting piece of the square, the second piece can have any of 16 possible positions. The third piece can have 20. The fourth can have 10. And any piece can have two inversions. The total number of arrangements necessary to try, therefore, is: 16 x 20 x 10 x 2—or *6,400.*

By the way, Mr. Mathematician, if you check this calculation and find it in error (on the low side, I suspect) please hesitate to write. I intentionally made only a quick, rough calculation, because that is the only kind needed to make the point.

Thus, if you averaged one trial every 15 seconds, trying all of the possibilities—without repeating any—this would take more than 26 hours, or more than *three normal working days!*

"But," perhaps you say, "this thing you called a 'problem' is really a *puzzle*—and a specially chosen one, at that, because it is *tricky*." And, in a sense, this is true—but misleadingly so. You will deceive yourself very badly indeed if you leave it at that, if you let this notion blind you to the deeper truth. For the plain reality is that *every problem in life is a tricky puzzle.*

If you think that this dinky little square problem is unusually complex and involved, check and see: exactly how many tricky elements are involved in buttons, bangles, books—or any of the other "simple" things in life.

Now, the object of all this, of course, is to show that once one has performed the pick-a-problem first step, the next intelligent move is *not* to plunge into a grasshopperish, cut-and-try, trial-and-error program. The trial-and-error method has its place (see Edisonian Method, page 85). But as a regular, habitual, standard, *primary* approach to creative problem-solving, it is entirely too tedious, inefficient—and on frequent occasion, downright wasteful and dangerous.

There is a better way. And that better way is . . .

Step 2: Get Knowledge

We can not think with what we do not know. Ideas never suddenly materialize out of nothing. Ideas are painstakingly *built,* assembled, manufactured out of some raw material. And that "raw material" is—*knowledge.*

Idea-building is very much like an atomic chain reaction in that each particle of information—or "fact"—in one's mind reacts and interacts with its neighboring bits to produce additional or new facts, thoughts, awarenesses, concepts, ideas.

By way of illustration—imagine that your mind were completely empty except for four bits of information. Then please note how very many possible thought-interactions you could have:

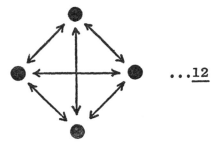

...<u>12</u>

Now, suppose you added just one more bit/fact . . .

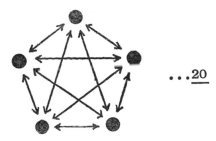

...<u>20</u>

Thus, the insertion of just one additional "fact-atom" into your mental "atomic reactor" does more than merely add to your idea-building capacity—it *multiplies* it!

How vitally important it is, then, to *get the facts* relevant to the problem. And it is easy, too, because we already thoroughly know what it means to "get the facts," don't we? (Goodness knows, this has been hammered into us for years; and, of course, the illustrations provided by certain popular TV detective programs have thoroughly clarified the importance and meaning of getting the facts.)

What?

By the way . . . What *is* a "fact"?

Take a few minutes here, get pencil and paper, and write out your definition of a "fact". State just exactly what a fact is, give several examples, and explain how you know your examples are facts. After you have done this, it will probably pay you to go on at least a little further, and check your thinking against the most authoritative sources or references you can find. Will do, please?

Most people, I find, when challenged to specify precisely what a fact is, start out with supreme confidence and respond with expressions such as "proven knowledge", "absolute truth", and so on. Soon, however, when they have begun to delve into the matter a little more deeply, particularly by giving examples and attempting to prove them, their certainty begins to fade and their statements begin to include expressions of much less cock-sure nature, such as "accepted", "belief", "inferred", "indicated", and the like. (You, too, I hope?)

Thank goodness this happens! Because, as a matter of fact (excuse the loose expression, please), there may not even *be* any such thing as a "fact"—not, at least, in the superficial connotation most of us seem to have in mind to begin with when we use the term. On the contrary, there may be only *evidences, assumptions* and the like—and these may be only tentative, at that.

Unavoidably, I suppose, we will go right on using the expression, "Get the facts." But for purposes of sound, creative thinking, we should use it always with inward thoughts of skepticism as to the real factuality, truth, genuineness, completeness and believability of our alleged facts.

How?

Now, that we're "sure" what facts are, the question becomes: *How* do we get them?

To a psychologist—and it is primarily a question of psychology in this context—the answer is: The only way on earth that we can receive information is *through our senses*. No matter what supplementary tools, aids or devices we use, information ultimately moves from object to mind, from outside to inside, via the basic senses of sight, hearing, touch, *et al*. (You can get quite fancy about this, too, if you like, by bringing in the senses of kinesthesia, temperature, pain, etc.)

The point is this: These sensory perceptors are the *only* natural equipment we have for "getting the facts", and our facts can only be as accurate as our receiving/perceiving equipment allows. And this equipment is fallible, indeed!

We could fill up the rest of this book with illustrations proving this point. But that would hardly be advisable. So if you feel that you must have immediate proof . . .

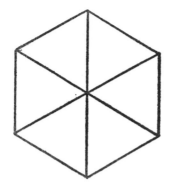 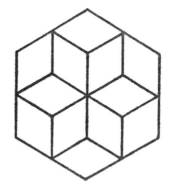

What do you see, above? On the left, do you see a sort of hexagonal pie—or a box—or what? On the right, do you see a six-pointed star in a frame—or a number of cubes, stacked one way and then another? Or, in both of the figures, do you see only certain arrangements of lines, sans any "depiction" or "interpretation"? Do you see what you see, or what you *believe* you see?

Now, if you *still* feel that your natural get-the-facts apparatus is nigh onto infallible, I suggest that you (1) check back on your performance in dealing with the Faulty-Observation-Inhibitor exercise, earlier in this book; (2) refer to "Illusion" in any good encyclopedia; and (3) visit the psychology department of your nearest university, and ask for a thorough test of your perceptual equipment.

Personally, I am continually finding that, just at those moments when I felt most positive I was comprehensively "getting the message", I was actually getting it only in distorted, garbled form, or perceiving only the existence of mere drops in the presence of the whole ocean.

And why, again, is it so all-fired important to check on the reliability of the evidence of our senses? Simply because, as a homespun philosopher once put it, "It ain't always what we don't know that gets us in trouble—sometimes it's what we 'know' that *ain't so.*"

Our facts, if they are to be useful as sound building blocks in the construction of new ideas, must be checked, double-checked, cross-checked, all-ways-checked—and *still* viewed as being subject to question. This attitude is characteristic of all true scientific thinkers, who are constantly suspecting and testing their own information, and who regard any "accepted" fact or theory as being only transient or tentative—that is, accepted only because of lack of evidence to *dis*prove it.

> By the way, is it perhaps a little clearer now why some people avoid thinking as the plague, and strive mightily to get through life with a simple, undemanding, comfortable set of opinions, prejudices or faiths, no matter how false these may really be?

Where?

Assuming for the moment that we have a fair insight into the matter of need for, nature of, etc., of these perverse, stubborn things called facts, the question becomes: *Where* can we get them?

In addition to the more or less obvious sources, I strongly recommend:

Reading. A single book ofttimes distills an entire *lifetime* of information-gathering. Further, it usually accomplishes this in such a way that the reader can grasp its essence in a matter of mere *hours*. (If "book-larnin' " education needs any defense— which it does not—is not this just about the most powerful argument imaginable?)

Listening. Listening, that is, to informed, knowledgeable people. And who might they be? Possibly everyone. For, as Emerson said, "Every man is my superior in some way. In that, I learn of him."

Oddly, some people seem to feel they are "lowering" or degrading themselves when they ask questions instead of trying to appear omniscient. But that is ridiculous. Because, as the old saying explains so well: "The fool will not learn, even from experience. But the wise man learns from the experience of *other* men."

Broad-field research. Which means directing your search for knowledge over a broad field rather than only a narrow specialty. It is impossible to determine at this stage just what information, or what kind and how much information, will be needed ultimately to build new ideas. But the broader your knowledge, the better your chances for sound success and the easier your task.

The suggestion of the use of wood for making paper, for instance, came not from a paper-chemistry specialist—but from an 18th-century naturalist observing wasps in action. And in a notable modern example, the "miracle drug" penicillin was discovered during research into what was seemingly a foreign field.

Wise, old C. F. Kettering even went so far as to say this: "I am afraid of specialists . . . and advise (potential innovators) to free themselves from categories, because basic truths have so much more in common than the specialists would have you believe. *All* branches of science overlap more than the guardians of special titles will admit . . ."

As you will learn sooner or later, if indeed you haven't learned it already, one of the special values of broad-field study and research is that it invites *"serendipity"*. And serendipity is deeply treasured by all experienced CT students, for the readily understandable reason that it is "the happy faculty of making discoveries—by accident or sagacity—which are not directly being sought."

*   *   *

In our efforts to gain knowledge, by whatever means, we find that it pays to be cautious about accepting so-called "expert testimony," especially if it has passed through a number of hands before reaching us. And we should be doubly skeptical about assertions of so-called fact that go, "Mr. C. D. Eksburtt, the renowned suchansuch authority, says . . ."—for these "facts" may not be valid at all. Mr. Eksburtt may be misquoted; he might be in error; possibly he was joking or exaggerating; and, all claims to the contrary, he may be decidedly *in*expert.

It is wise to keep in mind also that, among the leading authorities in any given field, there are almost always certain grave differences of opinion. Therefore, if even the most learned men can not agree on fundamental points, then we, too, would be well advised to accept their "facts" with reservations.

In all this fact-stockpiling activity, it is important to keep in mind the purpose of this step, which is to soak-up the raw material of idea-building: information. You should not yet be at all concerned with "new ideas" (at least, not beyond limited, tentative, speculative probings); for the new ideas will emerge later as a natural and inevitable consequence of your becoming steeped in knowledge—and *only* then.

There is just one key job to be done at this stage, and that is to learn all you can about the elements of the problem at hand. In short: *get knowledge.*

Summary

Step 2: Get Knowledge.

Get the known facts relevant to the problem. Get new knowledge. Study the written references on your subject. Experiment. Explore. Research deeply and broadly. Talk-with/question informed people.

Check your findings, to avoid being misled. Put them in writing.

Concentrate on getting information, not ideas, at this stage.

III. ORGANIZE KNOWLEDGE

It is no secret that work is accomplished more easily, satisfactorily and effectively when it is done systematically, in an orderly, organized way. And this applies no less to mental work than to physical work.

A revealing example of the importance of thoughtful, creative system is frequently seen in certain organizations at that (dreadful?) time when it is suddenly necessary to find a replacement for a key man who unexpectedly resigns, expires or for other reason precipitously departs the organization.

In the typical non-organized outfit, this is characteristically an occasion for tense, jittery, impulsive and expedient action. It is also an occasion, invariably, for immediate recourse to fallible human *memory*—or perhaps it would be more accurate to say *hasty recollection.* Small wonder that the outcome so often is the unhappy decision to hire on the outside, completely by-passing/overlooking exceptionally high-potential candidates already on the inside—but not remembered; or, worse yet, not even *known* except in a stereotyped sense. (". . . Make Whoozis a vice president? Are you off your rocker, or something? Why, he's a *personnel* man!")

In dramatic contrast to this is the organized concern wherein it was recognized matter-of-factly and long ago that people inevitably *will* move on, one way or another, despite the most fervent wishes that they might say put-and-35 forever. And this concern coolly, deliberately and calmly studies its manpower-potential in depth and with regularity—and does something by plan about *developing* manpower—so that, when a key-man move occurs, the concomitant replacement operation is managed soundly. And, while the whole thing may not be exactly "no sweat", it most assuredly is *minimum* sweat.

(By the way, if inadvertently I "tromped a nerve" just now, and this brings on the defensive response, "Those big outfits can afford elaborate programs; but we . . .," look out—it's a zillion to one you're rationalizing!)

After all of which discussion, now, it undoubtedly will come as no news item that the next step in our PakSA is . . .

Step 3: Organize Knowledge

Actually, this operation should no doubt be performed concurrently with Step 2. But whenever it is done, the important thing to keep in mind is this: To make the best use of our accumulated knowledge, for creative as well as any other kind of thinking—but *especially* for Creative Thinking—we need to sort it, classify it, put it into some intelligent order. Further, as shown by the foregoing manpower-replacement example, the importance and need for such sound organization increase critically in direct ratio with the complexity of the problem(s) to be solved.

As to methods of organizing knowledge . . . Depending upon the volume of information to be processed, Step 3 may be carried out with the aid of devices ranging from simple lists and outlines; through scrap books, ring binders, card indexes, etc.; to complete filing systems, microfilm libraries, punch-card systems, EDP tape, "keysort" outfits, and no doubt many, many others still "waiting" (opportunity for CT!) to be invented.

If you have ever read that near-classic of American humor,

Life in a Putty Knife Factory, you may recall that the author, H. Allen Smith, told how his book resulted from the simple habit of jotting notes of amusing little bits, incidents and observations on small scraps of paper and saving these scraps in an old cheese box on his desk. When he got enough scraps, he simply sorted them into the order he wanted (organized them, that is), then proceeded to write a "best-selling" new book from them.

Now, you may have no desire to create/write a new book. And that, of course, isn't the point of this illustration. The point is that, as an essential step in effectuating your preparation for creating original ideas—of whatever kind, and in whatever field —you will need to preserve your information in a form that will make sense to you and permit ready processing in succeeding steps.

In the final analysis, the matter is just this plain: If you make the mistake of slighting this operation, and merely accumulate a lot of miscellaneous information without organizing it, this will lead surely to chaotic jumble and confusion. (Oh, certainly, in working on some relatively simple problem, you might still finally manage to put together some sort of contrivance out of this mess—but at what an unnecessarily exorbitant price!) But if you give careful attention to this operation, the sense, clarity and comparative ease of the entire CT process will be tremendously increased for you.

Get your knowledge organized—in writing.

Summary

Step 3: Organize Knowledge.
Put your information into some sensible form.
Sort it. Classify it. Organize it.
Put it in writing.

PAUSE AND TAKE STOCK

You have been busy, these last dozen-and-more pages, and you may have lost some of the thread of continuity. So here it it again:
Step 1: Pick a Problem.
Define the problem—in writing.

First, state what's wrong—what needs fixing.
Second, state your objective—what end-result you seek.
Step 2: Get Knowledge.
Get the known facts relevant to the problem. Get new knowledge.
Study the written references on your subject. Experiment. Explore. Research deeply and broadly. Talk-with/question informed people.
Check your findings, to avoid being misled. Put them in writing. Concentrate on getting information, not ideas, at this stage.
Step 3: Organize Knowledge.
Put your information into some sensible form.
Sort it. Classify it. Organize it.
Put it in writing.
Implicit in these steps is the underlying knowledge that creation does not repeatedly, regularly and consistently occur and recur as a consequence of passivity, or of impulsive, aimless, disorganized action. Rather, it is the consequence of pursuant, active, thorough, systematic, persistent, self-disciplined, purposive *making-ready*. The pertinent principle, then, is this: *Creation comes out of preparation.*

Four Square

To test the validity of this "preparation:creation" principle, and the efficacy of the three relevant steps, I suggest that you apply them now to the four-part-square problem that you first encountered on page 126/127. Get some paper, a pencil, a rule, a protractor; and proceed . . .
Step 1: Pick a Problem. Define the problem and the objective in writing. (Go ahead and use the material on page 127, if you wish, because in this instance it is unlikely that much is to be gained from extensive re-wording.) Study your written statements for a moment, then go on.
Step 2: Get Knowledge. First, isolate the main elements of the problem, which in this case are: (1) the *pieces* of the square, and (2) the *square* which these pieces are to form.

Second, lay out two sheets of paper. On one, write the heading, "Square." On the other, write the heading, "Pieces."

Third, get the facts about the square and its parts. Measure and examine the pieces; and, on the appropriate sheet of paper, jot down the information you obtain. Assume whatever you can, sensibly, about the square (for example, each corner is a right angle), and write this down. (Note: Write down *every* bit of information you can obtain or reasonably assume—about this and *every* problem you undertake to solve creatively—because at this point it is impossible to know what information will be "significant" and what will not. [This can be known only *after* a problem is solved.] Many a valuable idea has remained unnecessarily unrevealed because its seekers have failed to investigate what they mistakenly presumed to be "too obvious" or "too trivial/unimportant" to warrant anything more than cursory examination.) Continue until you are satisfied that this step has been thoroughly completed.

Step 3: Organize Knowledge. Examine your lists of facts. Do you have items pertaining to size mixed in with items pertaining to shape, color and so on? If so, sort them out and separate them. Re-write your lists, then, putting together the items that belong together. Then sit back for a while and contemplate the meaning of your organized information.

Now . . . Go ahead, ad lib, relaxed, and solve the problem. Don't worry about "proper method" or "appropriate technique," etc., for now. Just go ahead and do "what comes natcherly."

And then . . . Study the experience you have just had, and compare it with the experience you had earlier with the same problem. Which of the two approaches accomplished the most the easiest—the grasshopper-like one or the ant-like one—the frenetic one or the organized one? What do you conclude?

Open-Ended

Now, before you go any further into the methodological details of the PackCorp Scientific Approach, you should carry at least one more practice project through—and somewhat beyond—the three preparatory steps. Why? Because, while these steps may have worked well in application to the four-part-square problem, which is primarily an analytical problem, it remains to be seen how effectively they work in the solution of problems of purely creative or many-many-possible-answer type.

Are you interested? Willing to give it a whirl? Good! Put PakSA to good use in this project:

Problem: Your wife, a thrifty woman, has for years made a habit of saving wire clothes hangers (beware of Label-Mindedness!) of the type commonly supplied by dry-cleaning establishments. She now has about 10,000 of them. She has steadfastly ignored your suggestions for getting rid of them, insisting that "They can be put to good use some day." Meanwhile, you need the space they now occupy in dead storage. Talking over the matter with your wife, you have finally got her to agree to let you move these tangled pieces of metal ". . . provided you don't just scrap them, but make them into practical objects, and find generally worthwhile uses for them."

Objective: Think up and list all of the "worthwhile uses" you can for these 10,000 objects.

Take it from there . . .

Apply Step 2—Get Knowledge:

Facts about the common wire clothes hanger:

About 3/32″ diameter, 42″ length . . .

Heavier than air, water . . .

Conducts heat, electricity . . .

Tensile strength is ....

Melts at .... degrees Fahrenheit . . .

Can be magnetized . . .

Springy, vibrates . . .

Is ductile, compressible, malleable . . .

Oxidizes, corrodes . . .

Combines/reacts with chemicals . . .

Fatigues readily . . .

Can be twisted, coiled, tapered, bent, flattened, sawed, stretched, painted, heated, chilled, welded, abraded, cut, bent, moved, moistened, dried . . .

———————————————————————
———————————————————————
———————————————————————
———————————————————————
———————————————————————
———————————————————————

Apply Step 3—Organize Knowledge: *ad lib.*
Go ahead . . . Meet the stated objective—again: *ad lib.*
And then . . . Take stock. *Now,* what do you conclude?

IV. REFINE KNOWLEDGE

' Occasionally, in applying the PakSA preparatory steps, one
may encounter one or two single facts of such apparent key importance that they seem to lead directly to the solution of the
problem at hand. But this can be a badly misleading impression,
because it leads us to believe that facts, *per se,* are the end-
object(s) of our search for insight, understanding, illumination,
inspiration; that it is these bits of information that *individually*
lead to new ideas.

Closer study shows, however, that the value of individual facts
is an *interim* value—that their value is as *links* in chains of
knowledge; that their purpose is to lead to the attainment of
something higher and more vital in the total Creative Thinking
entity.

The essential point at which I am aiming is this: Facts lead
to significant new ideas only as they lead to and through the discovery of certain *patterns.* And the discovery of these patterns
is brought about by applying . . .

Step 4: Refine Knowledge

Underlying this step is the fundamental thought that everything good in nature has design, consistency, integrity, pattern;
and that if we can discover what the particular patterns are in
a given CT-problem area, these patterns will in themselves—by
their very nature—provide the avenues to the new ideas we so
earnestly desire. In short, there is a higher scheme of things

that is the fountainhead of new ideas, and it is this scheme that we must fathom out.

As with any genuinely fundamental idea, this one is so basic and simple that it is difficult adequately to express and explain. But, to *try* to put it explicitly, precisely and concisely, it amounts to this:

FACTS

refined through the screens of

SIMILARITIES

DIFFERENCES

ANALOGIES

CAUSE AND EFFECT

lead to the revelation of certain consistent

RELATIONSHIP PATTERNS

which lead finally to the extraction of fundamental

PRINCIPLES AND LAWS

which reveal ways to build sound, new combinations or

NEW IDEAS

In brief: VARIABLES contain CONSTANTS which lead to NEW VARIABLES.

This is perhaps the simplest yet most deeply significant general idea in this whole book. For it is just this plain: *The only really reliable avenues to consistently sound Creative Thinking are Relationships and Principles.*

Reduced to its irreducible essence, therefore, this "super idea" means that the basic CT procedural plan is made up of just two operations:

1. *Gather material, take it apart, and find the core.* Find the "glue," the central scheme, the nucleus, the final denominator, that which ultimately holds the whole thing together in a sensible entity.

2. *Put it together again in a new and different way.* Rebuild it around the core in ways dictated by the nature of the *core*, not by the nature of the stuff around the core.

The Pyramid Pattern

To see the supreme sensibility of this idea, it helps to start by visualizing the pattern of man's thinking as conforming generally to the shape of a pyramid . . .

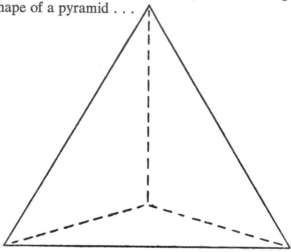

The base of the pyramid—the beginning of thinking and the lowest level of man's mental capability—is made up of *sense impressions* . . .

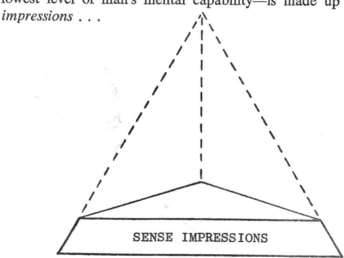

SENSE IMPRESSIONS

This is certainly not "thinking" as we customarily regard it. Nor is it thinking on a grand scale, for even the single-celled amoeba is capable of "thought" at this level. And, as you know, man's sensory equipment is by no means the keenest in the animal kingdom. Nonetheless, this *is* the start of all man's thinking, and the character and quality of the thinking done at this level very definitely influences the character and quality of the thinking done at higher levels. And, whether we are conscious of it or not, each of us is functioning constantly at this level throughout life—gathering and recording sense impressions by the million.

*   *   *

On the next higher level of thinking, man develops, from his sense impressions, certain *images* . . .

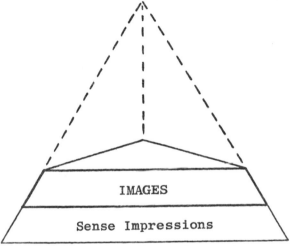

Out of some given number of sense impressions, one probably forms about one-tenth as many mental images. (Thus, out of a million sense impressions, one might form 100,000 images.) Vague, fuzzy, undefined, these images are little clearer than the first sensations one experiences when some person suddenly and unexpectedly shouts, *"Fire!"*

*   *   *

At the next higher level of thinking, out of his accumulated sense impressions and images, one forms certain *concepts* . . .

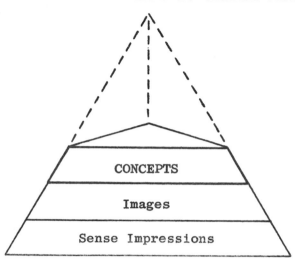

The dictionary defines a concept as "an organized unity corresponding to some universal; an idea comprehending the essential attributes of a class or logical species." Thus a concept is a kind of idea—but a very general one. For instance . . .

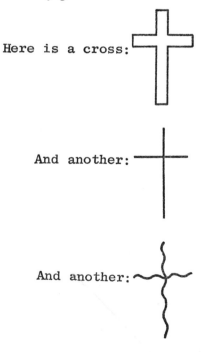

Each of these crosses is specific (an idea) and unlike the others. But each resembles the others, too, in that each conforms to a general design/concept wherein the "essential attributes" are a vertical line and a horizontal one.

So it is, at this level of thinking, that the mind classifies and organizes images according to broad, general, unifying concepts.

*   *   *

At the next higher level of thinking, a person further refines his concepts to form specific *ideas* . . .

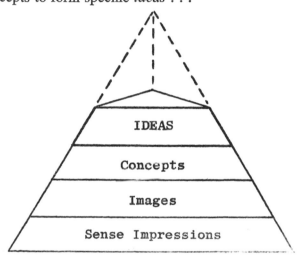

For example, continuing with the cross (shape) concept, this is the level at which one thinks, "Perhaps I could make a cross with a long horizontal line and a short vertical one. And (bringing in a different concept, now—one of *materials*) possibly it could be made of stone, or metal, or glass, or plastic, or fabric, etc. And (bringing in the concept of *color*) it might be white, or gold, or purple . . ." And so on.

So it is that concepts are the immediate parents of ideas.

> All right; I will agree: My pyramid is shaped wrong, for it ought to bulge outward again at this point. But the trouble is, I can neither draw this new figure to an accurate scale nor figure out a comprehensible name for it. So, if you will forgive this arbitrariness, I will just stick to my simple pyramid.

At the next higher level of thinking, one forms *judgments* . . .

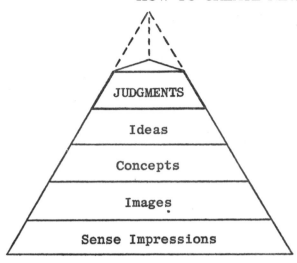

Following along again with the example of the cross, this is the level at which one is concerned with the evaluation of ideas, and thinks, "The bold-faced cross is better than the skinny one . . ." and so on.

This is also the level of thinking at which the monkeywrench all too often gets tossed into the machinery. For when thinking reaches *only* to the "judgment" level, the resulting judgments turn out about like this:

20% are *hasty,*
20% are *false,*
20% are *illogical,*
20% are *prejudiced,*
and only 20% are *sound.*

When thinking springs from the level above this one, however, the ensuing judgments turn out to be *90 to 100% sound.*

*   *   *

At the highest level of man's thinking are *principles and laws . . .*

The supreme value of principles and laws is that they *explain* so many things—not only in the area of present knowledge and understanding but, more importantly, *toward the creation of new ideas.*

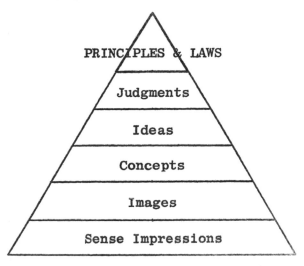

Do you want an example? Then imagine, if you can, the profound implications of this principle/law:

$$E = mc^2$$

Principle-level thinking leads, by its very nature, to both the soundest and most creative thinking of which man is capable.

Cases, Cases

The dictionary defines a principle as "A governing law which exercises a directing influence . . . ultimate basis or cause . . . a fundamental truth; a comprehensive law or doctrine from which others are derived or on which others are founded . . . a general truth . . . an elementary proposition or fundamental assumption . . . a postulate . . ."

> Since it is clear in this definition that, as between the two terms, "principle" and "law", the former is transcendental, hereafter I will use only the term *principle*—with the implicit understanding that it includes *law*.

But the definition hardly clarifies the matter, so we had better examine some cases.

You and I are interested in your *learning* effectively and thoroughly about the *Art and Science of Creative Thinking*. Accordingly . . .

Problem: It is vital to your success with the applied "A.S.C.T." that you remember and take into account certain key things concerning the inhibitor of CT called "Label-Mindedness." But there is great danger that you will *not* so remember (because, among other reasons, these key things are preceded and followed by a number of other ideas that are also "vital").

Objective: Vivify the information relevant to Label-Mindedness so that you will appreciate it, comprehend it, remember it, and use it to good advantage.

Principles: Two main principles of educational psychology came to mind:

1. *"If material to be learned is 'different' or 'unique,' it will be better remembered."*
2. *"A person will understand and remember that in which he is personally and actively involved better than that which he 'experiences' only in the abstract and impersonal."*

Idea: Take the most common material imaginable (paper); present it as a "glamorous," *new* material—that is, present it *un*commonly; then get you personally involved in a related creative exercise in such fashion that the exercise itself (and your experience with it, of course) impressively makes the point that your success in CT is greatly dependent upon your freedom from Label-Mindedness.

Did this idea solve the problem, meet the objective? Only you can tell, of course. But the odds are overwhelming that this idea was more successful than mere verbal exposition would have been—*because it sprang from sound principles.*

Bonanza!—while these two principles are fresh in mind: Isn't it perfectly obvious, now, that these so-called "principles of educational psychology" (please change label to *Principles of Human Behavior*) constitute a veritable mother lode of ideas of importance in many fields in addition to education? Suppose, for example, that your principal problem area is *safety,* or *advertising,* or *management,* or any other field wherein it is necessary and desirable to "get messages across." Don't these two potent principles directly suggest hundreds of sound ideas for attaining your objectives?

* * *

A few years ago, our whole national-defense program was threatened by a "bog-down" in *aviation* . . .

Problem: Millions of dollars and countless man-hours had been invested in the development of a certain advanced, dart-shaped, "supersonic" interceptor/fighter plane which, when tested, wouldn't even break through the sound barrier. No matter what power plants and other modifications were tried, the ship fell far short of performing at its design speed. Worse, other aircraft still in the design and development stage could be expected similarly to fail, because they were being patterned after this particular experimental ship.

Objective: (You state it:) _____

Principles: The project was about to be abandoned when a young aeronautical engineer recalled the *"Law of Avanzini":*

"A falling plate encounters resistance greatest at the center and least at the margin when it is falling vertically . . ."

Transposed (from "falling plates" to modified shapes moving through a relative wind, which would be the aerodynamic equivalent of "falling vertically") this principle suggested that Airplane X was being held back by a pressure build-up at its middle. And this was quickly verified in wind-tunnel tests.

Idea: Pinch-in the fuselage (body) of the airplane at its middle, thus making a place for the pressure to "go."

Result: The airplane *exceeded* its design speed, and led to even greater refinements and advancements. And you and I are a little safer than we were—and may one day fly more swiftly and economically ourselves because of the principle of a falling plate.

"How odd that this 'modern scientific breakthrough' derived from a principle nearly a century-and-a-half old," you say? On the contrary, how completely natural!

* * *

Any person who has any stake at all in business and industry (and who hasn't?) is vitally concerned with *communication* . . .

Problem: In a certain manufacturing concern, costs in recent years had been steadily rising. Management was particularly worried over the fact that employees were becoming more and more wasteful of the materials, when these constituted by far the company's largest cost of doing business. Company executives wrote letters to employees, held "Reduce Waste" contests, made appeals to the union, increased suggestion-system awards, printed special stories in the company newspaper, etc.; that is, they "communicated"—to no avail.

Objective: (Suppose you try your hand at spelling it out. Is the real and proper objective to reduce waste? Why? Cut costs? Why? Influence people? Why? Increase profits? Why?) _____

Principles: The president—so worried over this problem that he (luckily!) had even taken to reading some of the "long-haired" books in his company library—one day came across a seemingly innocuous little statement in a book having to do, in part, with motivation. "Dogma," he muttered to himself, and went on to other things. But that night, just as he was about to retire, the little statement returned to mind so sharply as to cause him to (1) exclaim to his wife, "Dogma, nothing— that's simple truth!" and (2) stay up half the night working on a plan to apply this "statement"/principle:

"People will learn only when they are listening; and they will listen only when what is said directly concerns them."

Idea: The president got the employees together in small groups, one group at a time, and said to them, "You are wasting yourself right out of a raise. And if you don't stop wasting soon, you will waste yourself right out of a job. Last month you wasted 19% of the material that passed to and through your hands. If you don't stop wasting you will be out of a job within a year, because the company will go broke by then. If you will cut waste by 10% or more—and hold it at that level or below for three months—I will then give you a 10¢-an-hour raise. Any questions? . . ."

Result: Waste was reduced to a "standard" 3½ %—and held there—within the month. The company was put back into "the black." The employees received *three* raises within the next 18 months. General quality improved. Prices to customers were reduced 7%. Orders increased. Productivity improved. Employment rose 25%. And everyone benefitted.

* * *

We could go on and on interminably here with cases in point. But that is neither necessary nor does it give you enough to do. So I have simply listed a few additional principles below; and I suggest that you see what you can do in the way of applying them to the creation of new ideas.

Economics: "Standard of living improves in proportion to increased productivity."

Philosophy: "Every change in nature is produced by some cause."

Management: "If a man is delegated the responsibility for accomplishing a result, he must be given authority to do so."

Chemistry: "Only those light rays which are absorbed produce chemical change."

Human Relations: "What a man does not understand, he opposes."

Optics: "When light falls upon a plane surface it is so reflected that the angle of reflection is equal to the angle of incidence, and the incident ray, and reflected ray, and normal all lie in the plane of incidence."

Design: "Form follows function."

Industrial Relations: ". . . A full day's work for a full day's pay."

It becomes increasingly clear, does it not?: Many good, new ideas *may* very well be generated at the embryonic level by concepts. But the soundest, most significant and most valuable new ideas are generated at the higher, refined level by the *super-*concepts called *principles.*

A Great Habit

Study of great creative thinkers shows that one of the principal reasons—if, indeed, not *the* principal reason—for their greatness lies in a simple habit they have in common: They are accustomed to thinking *beyond* facts—to find out what *underlies* facts and therefore what *transcends* them. They do not merely collect facts. They continually weigh, check, scan, review, cross-check, analyze, relate, combine, disassemble, classify, re-combine and inter-relate their facts in a constant effort to try to determine: *"What do they MEAN?"*

If you and I would emulate these great creative thinkers, then we, too, should cultivate this same habit.

Probably the most powerful single tool we can use for this purpose is—the *question*. Our basic tool kit contains the six questions: *Who? What? Where? When? How? WHY?* (We should be especially zealous about applying these questions to things that are as they are "because they've always been that way." Ex.: "The show must go on." *Why?*)

The most important question of all, however, is: *"SO WHAT?"* When all of the facts are in, *so what*—what can be *concluded* from them; what is the *central* idea or ideas they contain; what's "the nub" of the thing, the *kernel?*

This is your test for determining whether or not you have isolated principles. If you can state the relevant facts of a matter, then say, "Therefore . . ." and draw conclusions, you are most likely stating one or more principles. (Is it necessary to point out that your facts must be accurate and your conclusions must follow logically if your principles are to be right and true?)

Peter Drucker, an outstanding thinker, and almost incidentally a famous professor of management, once said, "The ability to summarize is the highest form of intelligence." He might also have said that this is the highest level of Creative Thinking, too—for it is.

Beware "Proverbial Poppycock"!

At this point, a special word of caution is in order: In our search for sound, basic, underlying, pertinent principles, we must *beware of cliches that masquerade as principles.* For, consider:

Long-current proverbs often come to be accepted as having great authority. They slide easily off the tongue, and they sound

profound—especially after having been repeated (and distorted?)
a few hundred times.

Many of these proverbs have "served" for generations. And,
because of the veneration in which they are held, they have even
gained a sort of sanctity. To deal critically with them might
seem almost sacrilegious. But truth has nothing to fear from
investigation—and investigation shows that many of these proverbs actually contradict each other.

For example, imagine a "Mr. A" and a "Mr. B," each armed
with a set of these sayings, and engaged in conversation. Their
dialogue might go like this:

A: Well, like I always say, "A penny saved is a penny
earned."

B: Perhaps so; but "You have to spend money to make
money."

A: You know, "Fools rush in where angels fear to tread."

B: I'm not so sure. "He who hesitates is lost."

A: It seems to me that "Everything comes to him who
waits."

B: Really? "Heaven never helps the man who will not act."

A: "A bird in the hand is worth two in the bush."

B: "Nothing ventured, nothing gained."

A: You know, of course, that "Two heads are better than
one."

B: Better—or just thicker? "Too many cooks spoil the
broth."

A: "A rolling stone gathers no moss."

B: "You get what you go after," and acquire polish in the
process.

A: "If you want a thing done well, do it yourself."

B: "A poor porter sweeps better than the best president."

A: Don't you know that "Nothing is sure but death and
taxes"?

B: The way I heard it, "The only certainty is change."

A: You talk entirely too much. "Silence is golden," you know.

B: "You can't say a kind word too soon, for you never know when it will be too late."

A: "When in Rome, do as the Romans do."

B: "Conformity is the easiest thing in the world; originality the most difficult and valuable." And "He who is content to 'be as the rest' has doomed himself to mediocrity."

A: "There is nothing new under the sun."

B: "The only adequate defense against the impact of a good, new idea is stupidity."

A: You'll have to admit, though, that "Ignorance is bliss."

B: "The more wisely a man thinks, and the more knowledge he acquires, the more he gains in capacity for work and enjoyment of life."

A: Everybody knows that "The purpose of business is to make money."

B: "He profits most who serves best."

A: You weren't paying attention. I said, "Business exists for profit."

B: I heard you, all right. "Money is useless except to serve people."

A: Everyone knows that "A rose by any other name would smell as sweet."

B: "Names and phrases are great makers of the things for which they stand."

A: Now, wait a minute. "Like father, like son."

B: How can that be? "Nature never duplicates."

A: You're too familiar with things. "Familiarity breeds contempt."

B: Come, now. "Nothing begets contempt like ignorance."

A: You move too fast, too—and "A rolling stone gathers no moss."

B : So you said before. But "Many a man has made a false step by standing still."

A : Well, now, you won't deny that "Experience is the best teacher."

B : "Every monkey has a lifetime of 'experience', but remains a monkey." And a Chinese philosopher once said, "One good lesson is worth a thousand 'experiences'."

A : Are you sure he didn't say, "One picture is worth a thousand words"?

B : Show me the picture that takes the place of *The Lord's Prayer*.

A : Say no more. I get the point: "It is twice as hard to crush a half-truth as a whole lie."

B : Amen, brother! And I salute you, for "A man who seeks truth and loves it must be reckoned precious to any human society."

Tools, Aids and Stimulators

Among the specific tools that are useful in this fourth step of our over-all PackCorp Scientific Approach, one of the most practical for bringing significant relationships to light, providing clues to guiding principles and thus leading to the production of new ideas, is the *check list*.

Here, for example, is a check list based upon Alex Osborn's now-famous principles of *adaptation, modification, magnification, minification, substitution, rearrangement,* and *reversal:*[1]

In what *new* ways could this (object, item, whatever) be used *as is?*
How could it be *changed* to suit a new use?
What *else* could be made from it?
How could the *waste/scrap/excess/by-product* be used?
Could the *shape* be changed to advantage?

---

[1] Material adapted from *Applied Imagination*, by Alex F. Osborn. Copyright 1953 and 1957 by Charles Scribner's Sons, 597 Fifth Avenue, New York, N. Y.

Suppose it were *curved, straight, tapered, twisted, coiled, flat?*

How about a different *package* or *combination?*

What about *motion, power?*

How about another *part/ingredient/material* in place of this?

Should it be *stronger, weaker?*

What might be *added, subtracted, divided, multiplied, proportioned?*

What about more *light,* or less, or a different *kind?*

How about different *sound,* or more, or less?

Could it be more *compact, condensed,* or *enlarged, expanded?*

Should it be *lighter, heavier, denser, less-dense?*

What about *spacing* it, *interrupting* it, putting it *together?*

Should it be *wet, dry?*

Should it be *streamlined, blunt, rough, smooth, shallow, deep?*

Could it be put into *assortments, assemblies, knock-downs?*

Should it be *exaggerated, understated, emphasized, toned-down?*

What about *speed, sequence, timing, frequency?*

How about an *alloy, ensemble, blend, isolated form, merger?*

What might be done to *attract the eye, tickle the taste, please the ear, improve the feel, sweeten the smell?*

Should it be *bigger, smaller, fatter, thinner, taller, shorter, narrower, wider, lower, higher?*

Suppose it were *rearranged; placed* differently; different *layout; raised, lowered, tilted, leveled, supported, suspended?*

What if it were *transposed, interposed, juxtaposed, superimposed, inside, outside, positive, negative, opposite, same, parallel, diagonal, up-ended, turned around, inside out, other-ended, slanted, angled, perpendicular?*

Doesn't this list suggest fascinating possibilities? And—be honest, now—doesn't it tempt you to say to yourself, "Let's forget all this baloney about 'inhibitors' and 'techniques' and 'principles' and stuff; because, man, this list is just what I've been waiting for!"

If this is the way you feel, and overpoweringly so, so be it. Go ahead and do what you feel you have to do.

Before you leave, though, do yourself a favor, will you?: Place a book-mark at this page; because you'll be back. Unless you are a mental flyweight (and you wouldn't have stuck it out this far if such were the case), this check list just won't prove to be *enough* for you. For the inescapable truth is that such aids are just that: *aids*, not substitutes for Creative Thinking. So get your fling over with as quickly as possible, will you? We've got some more foundation to build.

Now, aids such as this check list are of course most applicable to specific projects, situations or problems, and over the short haul. In order that you may secure broader and more long-term gains—that is, by building more enduringly helpful basic *habits* —I proffer and especially recommend two other imagination-stimulators:

Hobbies. Hobbies of both the collecting kind (stamps, coins, etc.) and of the making kind (painting, woodworking, etc.) are helpful. But the *most* beneficial hobbies are the latter —those wherein one first learns to apply the principles, tools and techniques developed by others before him, then proceeds to develop new ones of his own.

Games. Games of all kinds probably have some value. But the most valuable ones are those that require and involve highly active, imaginative mental play. (Roger Price's rib-tickler, "Droodles," is an excellent one on the light side, as are "Twenty Questions," and "Scrabble," and cryptograms, and others.) Best of all, I believe, are the so-called "brain teasers" and puzzles ("Thinker Toys," my friend John Triplett calls them), because they require and help to develop mental discipline and tenacity. Least helpful of all, in my acknowledgedly prejudiced estimation, are such stylized, rule-ridden games as chess and bridge, which have an unfortunate way of becoming grim ends unto themselves rather than aids to something greater.

The Other Eleven

In the event that you may have forgotten, temporarily: Besides the just-mentioned aids for stimulating the imagination and isolating/utilizing key relationships and principles, we have recourse also to the eleven CT techniques discussed earlier. Any of these techniques may be used, of course, either in more or less "pure" form or as adjuncts to the PackCorp Scientific Approach. In the latter primary application, however, I believe you will find these particular techniques to be most potent:

> Forced Relationship (obviously?)
> Gordon Technique
> Input-Output Technique
> Morphological Analysis
> Check-List Technique
> Attribute Listing

Summary

Step 4: Refine Knowledge.
Screen your information for Relationships and Principles.
> Match fact against fact; see what meanings they make together.
> Look for similarities, differences, analogies, cause-and-effect, combinations—patterns—concepts—principles—*ideas*.

SPECIAL FEATURE

Perhaps this section should have been included with the material on *Step 2—Get Knowledge,* since it has to do with the quality and character of the knowledge one secures. Or perhaps it is better suited for inclusion with the material on *Step 4—Refine Knowledge,* since it provides some illustration of the special value of principle-based thinking. Frankly, I couldn't make up my mind as to which placement was better. So, as you see, I have treated it as a sort of extra feature. In any case, I have extra-special reason to believe that you will find this deserving of special-extra study because of its value in helping to keep your thinking on a most high level of soundness and creativeness.

And what is this section all about? It is all about this:

When any one of us is endeavoring to develop creative solutions for problems of any magnitude, he finds it not only desirable but frequently imperative to seek facts, "raw material"—evidence—from sources and by means additionally to his own direct observations and investigations. That is, he seeks evidence from *others*. But if he chooses to regard such evidence with more than simple, blind credulity (as most certainly he should!), how can he determine whether or not the evidence so obtained is sound, valid, reliable, true?

A "situation," no?

Here, to help in this situation, are . . .

TEN PRINCIPLES FOR GAUGING THE SOUNDNESS OF EVIDENCE

1. *The Principle of* AUTHORSHIP:
   Who and what is the author? What is his background, association, education, experience, training, position, reputation, character? Can he be regarded normally as a competent observer and reasoner? Do his special abilities as an observer and thinker apply in this particular situation?

2. *The Principle of* MEDIUM OF EXPRESSION:
   In what kind of publication does the author's presentation appear? In the case of oral expression, where, when, under what circumstances and on what occasion was the presentation made? If the statements appear in a newspaper, magazine, journal, pamphlet or book, who are the publishers and owners—and what is their reputation and known bias, if any?

3. *The Principle of* MOTIVATION:
   Is the author or speaker presenting his arguments and conclusions because he sincerely believes in their truth, merit and importance for others? Or, rather, is he acting merely as the hired servant of some axe-grinding person, group, institution or nation? What motives seem to in-

spire and direct his arguments? Are these motives frankly, truly and fully stated or otherwise clearly indicated, or must they be inferred?

4. *The Principle of* RELIABILITY:
Are the "facts" that are presented *real* facts, or are they pseudo-facts or distortions manufactured by the writer or speaker? If they are genuine facts, what evidence is presented or available to prove them? If statistics are quoted, are they given *sans* manipulation, and is their source stated with adequate supporting information about the nature of the statistical study cited—or, instead, is there an attempt to "lie with statistics"?

5. *The Principle of* SUFFICIENCY:
Are there *enough* proven facts and sound reasons presented to make each general conclusion credible? Is there positive support for the arguments advanced, and not merely a shifting of the burden of proof? Do the assertions rest upon selected instances or hasty generalizations? If only opinions or personal faiths are being expressed, is this made clear?

6. *The Principle of* INTERNAL CONSISTENCY:
Does the speaker or writer contradict himself by stating different conclusions about the same topic in different parts of his presentation? Is there any evidence of "special pleading," or the treatment of similar situations in dissimilar ways for reasons of personal or group advantage?

7. *The Principle of* IMPARTIALITY:
Where there is issue, have the arguments of the *other* side been honestly stated and clearly answered? Or have they been presented in distorted or exaggerated form— and belittled or ridiculed rather than analyzed?

8. *The Principle of* COMPREHENSIVENESS:
If there has not been time or space enough for thorough discussion of opposing views, have these views at least been treated with courtesy and respect, and not just denounced or subtly disparaged?

9. *The Principle of* SOUND DEDUCTION:
   Do the conclusions that are drawn *really* follow necessarily from the evidence and reasoning advanced? Can *other* conclusions be reached from the same evidence?

10. *The Principle of* SOUND PREDICTION:
    Are the predicted consequences really certain—or fairly probable—or merely possible? In any case, what scientifically acceptable evidence is presented or cited to support the predictions?

NOT QUITE ALL

At this *Step 4* stage, the new ideas start forming—or, at least, they should—slowly at first, perhaps, then at an accelerating rate. And when this happens, of course, you are pleasantly on your way to attaining your objectives.

But sometimes, the ideas—perverse things!—seem stubbornly to *refuse* to emerge. You concentrate on the problem; you study intently; you apply mental pressure—and simply block, frustrate, come grinding up against a dead end. Or you find you can produce only the most hackneyed, superficial, unoriginal ideas— great, big, fat nothingnesses.

Unusual? Not at all. To a slight or severe degree, or any degree in between, this happens almost standardly, it seems, to *everyone* who endeavors to deal creatively with difficult problems of serious import, magnitude and consequence. There is small comfort in this knowledge, however. And furthermore, it isn't even very important to know at all. For the only thing that *really* counts in this situation is—*what then?* And here is "what then":

When you "blank out" in the manner just described, the first logical action is to re-trace your steps . . .

Re-define your problem. Originally you may not have conceived the problem clearly. Or it may be necessary and desirable to re-state it in the light of new insight gained in the process of seeking, gathering, organizing and refining your information. Or you may even discover that you have been working on the wrong problem!

Re-study your information. Your facts may be false,

wrongly interpreted, misapplied, over- or under-emphasized, out of context, disorganized, or otherwise inadequate or incomplete.

Re-screen your knowledge for significant relationships and principles. Question. Rearrange. Look closer. Challenge. Step back to get perspective. Shake something loose. Look for "odd-ball" clues. Check your basic assumptions and premises. See what fits and what doesn't. Re-examine for similarities, differences, analogies, cause-and-effect, combinations, patterns, concepts and principles.

And if, after all this, the problem remains opaque and the ideas *still* are slow in coming to mind . . .

V. Digest

Science now generally accepts, and appears to have confirmed, what many earlier students such as Freud, Jung, Adler, *et al,* long believed alone—namely, that man has, in addition to a consciousness, some sort of *subconscious* mind; further, that the subconscious mind is one over which man exercises little or no direct control but which, in some way, very definitely influences him and his thinking.

No one professes to understand the exact, mysterious processes by which the subconscious functions. And, fortunately for our purposes here, such understanding not only is not a make-or-break matter; it is highly questionable whether possession of such intimate physio-bio-chemical information would contribute very importantly to the utilization of this mental function. The practical need, as opposed to the academic one, is to know: just what is the *effect* of the subconscious and, if it can be used at all in a purposive, controlled way, *how* can it be so used? And in this we are in luck.

In CT, the subconscious apparently has two special and much-to-the-point abilities: First, the ability to "take over" and continue working on a problem when the conscious mind is blocked, or fatigued, or unable to concentrate effectively—or, in short, is "getting nowhere fast." Second, the ability to process mental food, or information, in much the same manner as the body processes material food—that is, by separating the bulk into a variety of substances, discarding some, modifying some, and saving and using that which is of consequence.

Since this is so, the obviously intelligent thing to do is: *use it* —carry out . . .

Step 5: Digest

The procedure for applying this step is simplicity itself: Take the "stewpot" off the "front burner"; put it on the "back burner"; and let it "simmer." Or, to use an athletic metaphor—give the conscious mind a chance to catch its "second wind"; let it refresh itself while the subconscious mulls over the problem.

Does this mean that, every time you feel you are making slight (if any) headway with a problem, you should stop work? Not at all. Quite often it is found that the smartest thing to do at this point is: simply drop the "stymied" problem, temporarily—and go to work on a *different* problem.

If you have become *completely* dead-ended/"fagged"/stalled, however, this course is in order:

Change activities altogether—from mental to physical. This is not only good for your general health; it will also help to keep you from harmfully "batting your head against a wall" or engaging in other exercises in futility.

Relax—with some routine, undemanding work. This, too, is good for the general health—and it also contributes to the noble aim of trying to get *all* of one's work done.

Rest. The chances are, you have used up your "current", and you need to pause a little while to let your batteries re-charge.

Recreate. Walk; listen to music; play; read (light material, preferably); see a show; travel; enjoy some mild diversion— until (as explained in the original-but-popularly-forgotten definition of the term, "recreate") you are genuinely re-animated, re-energized, given fresh life.

A Larger Value

Now, perhaps it would be wise to pause here and consider a trio of possible dangers connected with *Step 5—Digest:*

First, there is the danger of misapplying it through rationalization. That is, one needs to be wary that he is not simply going in for self-deception by skipping hastily to this step—which is easy—and not doing an honest job of working out the preceding steps—which is not so easy.

Second, there is the danger that one may misconstrue (purposely?) the term "digestion" in some twisted way to infer "*ingestion*"—that is, specifically, ingestion of alcohol. This may lead to "refreshment" of a sort, but to imbibe so in the belief that CT output varies upward and directly in ratio with alcoholic input is a most dangerous sort of foolishness. The notion persists popularly, I have been sorry to learn, that artists, writers, composers and other innovators habitually do fine creative work while loaded with "booze"—the "logical" conclusion being, therefore, that alcohol is a stimulant. But, in plain, demonstrable truth, the diametric *opposite* is the case: Drunks create a hundred times more problems than solutions. And alcohol is not a stimulant; it is a *depressant*—it *inhibits* creative ability. As for genuine stimulants, some of them may provide a temporary lift to CT; but research has shown that only wholesome activities and rest provide truly effective, lasting re-energization.

Third, there is the danger of so emphasizing the importance of digesting at those times when the idea-generating going is rough as to obscure the importance of this step when the going is comparatively smooth and easy. Truth is, Step 5 should be carried out in *either* event. Why? There are at least three important "becauses":

1. Even when the ideas are literally pouring out, these first ones (remember?) are practically never the best ones that a person is capable of producing. They are, on the contrary, ones that usually have to be gotten out and out of the way to clear the path for the *genuinely* best, unique ones to follow—that is, to follow digestion.

2. A person *always* produces more and better ideas in "PakSA-ing" a CT problem, not by carrying out Steps 1, 2, 3, 4 and 5 just one time, but by carrying them through *repeatedly.*

3. Every person *always* has at least several more good ideas

left in his idea-reservoir—even when he believes that this tank has been drained—and the process of mental digestion brings them to the surface of the consciousness.

Summary

Step 5: Digest.

Remove the problem from your mind's "front burner" to its "back burner."

Let your conscious mind get a "second wind"; let your subconscious work on the problem.

Take up another problem, or relax, or work at a hobby, or enjoy some mild diversion—until refreshed.

VI. PRODUCE IDEAS

Now, if one has done an adequate job of working out each of the PakSA steps up to this point, a strange and wonderful phenomenon inevitably occurs:

There is a sudden emergence of *insight,* or *inspiration,* or whatever you wish to call it. Surprisingly, and seemingly all at once, without any necessarily apparent leading-up-to-it, the problem is clarified in the light of a remarkable sort of *illumination.* Further, this clarification generally strikes—almost literally, "strikes", with a nearly physical impact—at a most unexpected time and/or a most unexpected place. It might occur during a meal, or when one is just idly musing, or during a bath. It might even strike with such impact as to waken one from a sound sleep.

Relaxation, curiously—particularly the relaxation just at the apparent point of completion of the Step-5 or mental-digestion cycle—evidently serves the function of "triggering" this breakthrough, this effect described by John Dewey as a "leap in thought".

Mozart, for instance, said that the theme of his *Magic Flute* came to him while he was playing billiards. The chemist Kekulé conceived his theory of atomic groupings when, riding one day on top of a London bus, he "saw the atoms dancing in mid-air". Berlioz was bathing in the Tiber when he suddenly found himself humming a musical phrase that he had long sought in vain. James Watt, while walking to a golf house, saw in a flash how waste of heat in a steam engine could be reduced by condensing steam. And the mathematician Poincaré established the identicality of certain "Fuchsian functions" with non-Euclidian geometry—again, "in a flash"—while on a geologic excursion, and without anything in his immediately preceding thoughts seeming to have paved the way for it.

But if such spectacularly spontaneous "sparking" does *not* occur in exactly this way—"naturally", and seemingly of its own volition—following Step-5 refreshment, one simply puts his conscious mind back to work on the problem, then finds it amazingly easy to perform . . .

Step 6: Produce Ideas

So be assured: however this may happen, it *will* happen. In dealing with any of your particular, well-defined creative problems—

If you have gathered together enough of the right facts . . .

If you have organized your facts intelligently . . .

If you have refined your information thoroughly, and isolated, extracted and articulated the consanguine relationships and principles . . . and

If you have provided for good mental digestion . . .

. . . have no doubts about it—some sort of significant *idea* will emerge, and it will be followed by others in rapid succession.

This, of course, is the end toward which you looked forward from the moment of undertaking to solve your problem creatively in the first place. But this is *not* "the end". For (among other reasons) peculiarly, when you arrive at this stage, you may find a totally unanticipated new difficulty:

Once the ideas begin to emerge, they practically tumble out upon each other. They begin flowing so fast that the memory can not absorb them all. Further, some of them may be so fleeting and evanescent that they seem to *dis*appear as mysteriously as they appeared. Thus, many of these transient, fragmentary ideas—quite possibly the *best* ones—may be lost!

Possibly the best simple technique yet invented for capturing these elusive, will-o'-the-wisp ideas is, simply: *put pencil to paper.* (The pertinent old saying, "A short pencil will beat a long memory," has solid foundation in two principles of learning—that of *repetition,* and that of *multiple sense impression.*) A sudden flood of new ideas may be expected to catch a person unawares on occasion, but there is no reason why it must necessarily catch him unprepared to react appropriately.

The point is obvious, no?: You should *expect* new ideas to come along in surges. Therefore you should spot recording materials where you can quickly put them to use. And, when those ideas begin to smack you 'tween the eyes—*get 'em down!*

Study and experience have shown further that, at this stage, it is imperative to refrain from stopping to judge one's new ideas. Instead, all resources should be concentrated on the production of as many alternative ideas as possible. Creation needs to be seized at the flood; evaluation should be subsequent, never concurrent.

So keep 'em coming. Then—and only then—when the supply is exhausted, or you are otherwise satisfied that it is time to go on, proceed to the next step.

Summary

Step 6: Produce Ideas—ad lib, or . . .
Concentrate anew on your problem until ideas begin to emerge. As they occur, don't stop to judge them. Just produce them, and record them. Build up as many alternatives as you can.

VII. Re-work Ideas

There is a deep and genuine thrill in creating new ideas. (Certainly, it is frequently bone-wearying, tension-filled, up-hill work; but in the end . . .) It is, in truth, just about the most exalting experience that a mere, mortal human can have.

But, unhappily, this very head-in-the-clouds feeling can also be the undoing of many a creative person and many a valuable new idea. For the new-idea-creator's impulse, upon getting that "Eureka!" feeling, is to bubble over, to yip and jump and shout the glories of his accomplishment from the roof-tops. He wants to rush out immediately, button-hole a prospective idea-buyer (or, on occasion, anyone who is available) and show off his new baby. And you know what happens then—the supposed "buyer", a normal human being who is insensately put on the defensive by this surprising, aggressively over-enthusiastic outburst, immediately resists.

Quite often, the irritated "prospective buyer" so resents the imposition of the hopped-up announcement of the new idea upon him that he not only resists accepting it; he *attacks the idea.*

And usually it is fairly easy to justify such an attack—because a new idea, fresh out of the "lab", almost invariably *does* have flaws. Indeed, most (if not all) new ideas come to mind well before they can be logically justified or reasonably explained. (An extreme example of this was one of Sir Isaac Newton's discoveries—on the roots of equations—which was proved *200 years* after it first occurred to Newton!)

So a real problem in self-discipline occurs at this point: the father of the new idea has to simmer down and force himself to *reason,* not merely feel.

Just about the smartest thing that "Dad" can do in this situation is firmly set aside the new idea, temporarily, and get busy with something else. Then, when he returns more calmly to the idea, he is generally able to view it more nearly as though he is seeing it through the eyes of a dispassionate stranger. Thus he can be considerably more detached, impersonal and objective in evaluating the idea.

If he then finds the idea to be fundamentally unsound—that is, when checked against the criteria of his own earlier-stated objectives—he can discard it, thereby saving himself wasted time, effort and resources, and preventing possible embarrassment. If, on the other hand, he finds that the idea holds up basically under critical scrutiny, he can see its correctible imperfections clearly and rationally; and then he can more easily and thoughtfully go about the job of doing the reshaping, modifying and re-working necessary to correct his idea's flaws, and make it work.

Common Failure

The importance of this step can hardly be over-emphasized.

An idea that exists only in nebulous, incompletely-worked-out form stands hardly a chigger's chance of gaining even tentative acceptance, let alone of ever bringing about any worthwhile human benefit. Quite the opposite—its greatest chance is of having minds slammed shut in its face, thus doing it to death.

If sometime you feel tempted to slight this operation, I am deeply hopeful that you will first remember to turn once more to this page and consider . . .

Scientific probing in depth of the subject of creativity repeatedly reveals, among other things, this constant:

> *The most common cause of failure among innovators is failure to follow ideas through to testing, verification, modification and development into final, workable form.*

Not lack of ability. Not lack of basically good ideas. Not any other lack but *failure to follow through* is the most common failure in Creative Thinking.

Summary

Step 7: Re-work Ideas.

Check your enthusiasm until you have checked your new ideas for flaws. Examine each idea objectively. Question it; challenge it; improve it.

VIII. PUT IDEAS TO WORK

When one has tested, verified, re-worked and developed his ideas into what he believes is workable form, plainly it is time for . . .

Step 8: Put Ideas to Work

If one has been successful in his CT efforts up to this point, it may appear that now—at last!—he can relax. ("The game's over and we won, Mom.") He can sit back, now, and let the world beat the proverbial path to his door.

No? No. Would that this were so, perhaps, but it isn't.

As we seem to keep discovering, every time we come upon what looks to be a simple and easy step in the PakSA procedure, the surface appearance is usually deceptive. And this is certainly true of Step 8. When we dig beneath its surface, we find that the successful completion of this step may involve as many as *three* important sub-operations.

We had better look into them . . .

A: Decide WHICH Alternatives

I have no way of knowing whether or not you have been aware of it; but, whether you have or not, the truth remains that I have been intentionally guilty of permitting two strong inferences to lie tacitly between the lines of my presentation thus far. To lay these inferences *on* the line, now, they are:

Inference 1: It is always possible to "get all the facts" (and relationships and principles, *et al*) needed to create worthwhile new ideas.

Inference 2: Using certain techniques and tools and systems and formulas and methods, the creation of successful new ideas (*re* any given problem) is virtually a sure thing.

And neither of these inferences is quite correct.

Re the first one: We sometimes *must* proceed basically by "making reasonable assumptions", "playing hunches", "taking educated guesses", and the like—for a variety of reasons. Key facts may simply be unobtainable; time may be too short, as when one must meet a deadline not of his own choosing; and so on.

Re the second one: The final outcome of CT is *always* uncertain, unpredictable. Furthermore, as Professor Edward Hodnett points out in his excellent book, *The Art of Problem Solving*, "Only in the wonder world of mathematics do problems have perfect solutions."[1] And, sometimes, certain ideas can not be tested at all—except the *first* time.

---

[1] From *The Art of Problem Solving*, by Edward Hodnett. Copyright 1955 by Harper & Brothers, 49 East 33rd Street, New York, N. Y.

There is more to the matter than this, too; but I'm sure you get the point: A CTer frequently finds himself, at or about this stage, in possession of a number of alternative ideas, some of which may succeed quite readily, some of which stand considerably less chance of success, and some of which may be quite risky indeed. And this can be the case regardless even of the real, intrinsic merits of the ideas.

So, since he is faced with all these "mays", the CTer is also faced with a decision—*which* alternative ideas should he "put to work"?

There are at least five general approaches that one might follow in deciding which of his ideas to put to work:

1. *Saturation Approach.* Perhaps it would really be more fitting to call this a "no-decision approach", because in applying it one plays no favorites among his ideas but simply tries to put *all* of them to work in the hope that "natural" or sink-or-swim processes will take care of the whole question of decision. Needless to explain, this is a highly hazardous approach. Nonetheless, it is a common one; and, at times, it may also be a necessary one.

2. *Intuitive Approach.* In effect, this is a sort of "digestive" or "free association" approach consisting principally of mulling and mulling and mulling until the subconscious pushes a decision or decisions to the surface of the mind. Judging by the results of certain survey studies of the subject of *Leadership,* the likelihood appears to be that this is *the* classic or standard method used by the majority of highpowered (and highly successful) executives and others whose main job is to make decisions. The fact that these people testify that they need to be only consistently 52-plus percent "right" to be successful is perhaps an indication of the reliability of this approach.

3. *Ranking Approach.* In this approach, one first attempts to establish certain criteria (objectives, principles?) which appear to have pivotal importance in the situation at hand. Then he ranks his ideas according to how they "stack up" against these criteria. For example, if a typical factor or criterion should be, let's say, *"Radicality,"* or *"Degree of Change,"* one might say to himself, "Idea X will involve the slightest change in the particular situation at hand, so I'll rank it as 'Number One'; Idea Z

will involve the most radical change, so I'll rank it last . . ." and so on.

The most serious difficulty in this approach, of course, lies in the determination of the significance or validity of one's criteria—and this can be a serious difficulty, indeed.

4. *Known-Odds Approach.* The essential feature of this method is simply that one chooses relatively known odds over the unknown. Thus, in effect, he says to himself, "According to all the evidence I have—incomplete though I understand it to be—Idea A has a better chance of succeeding than has Idea B."

The decision made by former President (then General) Eisenhower on the Normandy Beach invasion of World War II is a famous example of this approach. "Ike" knew that the odds were in favor of a short period of passable weather on the pre-set D-Day, following which there would very likely be an indefinite period of quite bad weather. So he launched the invasion and caught the enemy by surprise. (Historians have since said that had Eisenhower not made this decision, it would have been necessary to delay the invasion for a full year—after which time the chances of getting a relatively easy success would have been greatly reduced.)

5. *Statistical-Analysis Approach.* If the necessary information exists—and that is the big question upon which this whole approach rests—undoubtedly the best long-haul way to "crystal-ball" one's alternative ideas is to figure the mathematical expectation. There are all sorts of complex statistical procedures and machineries for doing this to a "T". But it can also be done simply—and with a workable degree of accuracy, too—by applying the basic formula . . .

$$W \times f/n, \text{ or}$$

$$\text{Winnings} \times \frac{f \text{ (number of possible FAVORABLE outcomes)}}{n \text{ (TOTAL number of possible outcomes)}}$$

For example, suppose you had three alternative new products, each with an apparent profit-potential of $1,000,000 a year. After conducting a careful customer-reaction study, however, you found that typical, prospective buyers reacted to your new products in these ratios: 134 out of a thousand favored Product

#1; 386 out of a thousand preferred Product #2; and 520 out of a thousand liked Product #3 best. Thus, if it could be assumed that this is the only consideration to be taken into account (which is an over-simplification excusable only because this is an illustration only as to the *kind* of calculation involved in this approach), the *probable* profit-potential per year of your respective new products is something like this:

Product #1: $1,000,000 × 134/1,000 — or *$134,000*
Product #2: $1,000,000 × 386/1,000 — or *$386,000*
Product #3: $1,000,000 × 520/1,000 — or *$520,000*

Now, each of these remains a gamble, and you *still* must make some decision, of course. But having sampled the odds, as above, you can feel relatively better assured as to the probable outcome of whatever gamble you decide to take.

And now, somewhat unhappily, I am going to have to leave the whole subject of Decision at this. It is a critically important subject in its own right, I must admit. And I must also admit that it is much, much too big and ramified to be treated with adequacy here, even if I were qualified to so treat it (which I am not) and there were space enough (which there is not). Pretty obviously, therefore, I must recommend that you consult other sources of information on the subject. To start with, I especially recommend two such sources:

Every Day Is Doomsday (article), Lydia Strong; Management Review; American Management Association; November, 1955.

The Art of Problem Solving (book), Edward Hodnett; Harper & Brothers; 1955.

B: Sell

If the situation is such that you can put your new ideas into use without having to deal with, involve or consult anyone else, then you are "in like Flynn", of course; and you can ignore this *Operation B: Sell.*

Chances are, however, that most of your ideas will involve others in some way; so you will have to do a careful job of selling in order to get acceptance of your ideas. And this can sometimes be the most difficult of all the CT jobs—because people practically never leap quickly and enthusiastically to acceptance of new ideas. Typically, on the contrary, they invariably react initially to the new and different in this fashion:

"We've always done it this way."
"You can't argue with success."
"It's never been tried before."
"It's against company policy."
"We'll be the laughing stock."
"We've done OK without it."
"That's not our job."
"Unrealistic!"
"Too idealistic!"
"Our place is different."
"It isn't in the budget."
"Let's form a committee."
"We're too busy for that."
"It's too much trouble to change."
"Management will never go for it."
"But we've *always* done it this way!"

Natural, typical or common though such resistance may be, however, the fact remains that people *do* accept new ideas— when *impelled* to do so—else we would have no progress at all. And, from studying some of the best of the mountain of literature on the art and/or science of selling, from observing highly successful idea-salesmen in action, and from personal experimentation and experience, I have come to the conviction that the consistently successful selling of new ideas is intimately wrapped up in principles of *Preparation, Gestation, Participation, Illustration* and *Orientation*. To put these principles into brief rule form . . .

1. *Plan Your Sale* (Preparation)—Assemble all the selling points (benefits, attributes, advantages) for each new idea, and decide in advance exactly how, to whom, when and where you will present each one.

2. *Allow Enough Time* (Gestation)—Many people are made uncomfortable by new ideas. If you try to rush them, you may never get them to buy. It takes time to *get* new ideas; and it takes time to get *used* to them, too.

3. *Get Participation* (Participation)—Our human tendency

is to be jealous of our accomplishments and to resent others' tampering with our creations. But, invariably, best results are obtained by *encouraging* discussion of the "pro's and con's" of new ideas. So, allow some voice in decisions concerning them—necessary modifications, how they shall be used, etc. Best of all, if you can possibly arrange it, is to get participation in *development,* for those who own a share of a new idea are just as eager as you are to see it succeed.

4. *Use "Samples"* (Illustration)—Successful salesmen know that the showing of their products is often the key factor in making the buyers want to buy. In your case the "products" may be intangibles, but the principle still applies. So *show, demonstrate* and *illustrate* your ideas. Depict them with action, sketches, charts, models, pictures, mock-ups—whatever will let your prospective customers *see* their merits and say, "Sold."

A special note: Whatever you use to help visualize any of your ideas, *make it neat.* A messy, careless, sloppy job always implies messy, careless, sloppy thinking. But a neat job says, more eloquently (albeit subtly) than words, "The originator of this work has put careful thought into it."

5. *Stress CUSTOMER Interest* (Orientation)—Unflattering as this harsh truth may be, it is nonetheless true that the other fellow is not half as much interested in you or your ideas as he is in himself and his problems. *Use* this knowledge, then: Soft-pedal your connection with the ideas at hand. Instead, concentrate on showing your prospective customer the only thing he really cares about—what, if anything, your ideas will do for *him.*

C: Teach

A wise observer once said, "Every time a man puts across a new idea, he finds a hundred men who thought of it before he did—but they only *thought* about it."

The difficulty of selling new ideas may partially explain the ineffectuality of these "hundred men." But perhaps a relevant personal experience will make it a great deal clearer. So, if you will, please, get paper and pencil and a watch, and carry out this exercise:

1. Write your full, complete, legal name, just as you normally do—and time the operation.

2. Now, write your name again—this time, however, writing only *every other letter* of your name—and time the operation.
3. Compare the results of these two operations. What do you observe? What does it signify? What do you conclude?

In my own experimentation with this little exercise, and others of the same kind, I have found that the average person requires twice as much time to complete the second operation as to complete the first—that is, *he takes twice as long to do half as much work!* (Is this about what you found, too?)   The logical conclusion, therefore, must be that whenever a person is given simpler methods of performing his work, as by a benevolent Management, it is inevitable that he will immediately start "dogging it", because that is the nature of the average person—especially the average employee—stubborn, lazy, uncooperative, and that is all there is to it.

But *is* this the correct, "logical" conclusion, albeit a common one? Is this *really* "all there is to it"? No, *no, NO!*

To get right to the point . . .

In most cases—certainly so in business and industry—new ideas also inevitably involve new *methods*. And, peculiarly, many people (and this includes many CTers) seem not to realize that when a method change is undertaken, the task of getting it installed and put into actual, regular, standard, habitual, proper use requires a great deal more than "gentle persuasion" or selling.

What many fail to comprehend is that even when a person willingly and whole-heartedly *tries* to adopt a new method in place of an old and familiar one, he is severely handicapped by "priority controls"—by neurological, physiological, pathological and psychological controls—controls that neither developed overnight nor can be altered overnight. Manifestly, the person's *unconscious habit patterns* are upset by the new and different methods. His *automatic skills* are disrupted, interfered with. *Emotional conflicts* frequently are set up; and these can be so severe (especially with older people) as to cause traumatic damage, or "nervous breakdown".

This certainly means one thing: Careful, patient, skillful, sustained *teaching* is required. Make no mistake about this. Controlled instruction with supervised practice over an extended period is not just "desirable". It is nothing less than *imperative*— else the person trying to perform the new method will surely regress, and one more "idea man" will unhappily and needlessly find himself to be just an ordinary member of the multitude who "only thought" and never accomplished.

Summary

Step 8: Put Ideas to Work.

Decide which alternative ideas to put to work.

If the approval and acceptance of others are required, sell your ideas.

> Plan each sale—decide the how/who/when/where in advance.
>
> Allow enough time—don't try to rush or push.
>
> Get participation—let others own a share so they'll help, not hinder.
>
> Use "samples"—visualize each idea; show/demonstrate/illustrate.
>
> Stress *customer* interest—soft-pedal the "I"; stress the "You."

If new methods and skills are involved, teach them.

IX. REPEAT THE PROCESS

Now—at last!—if you have done well in carrying out Steps 1, 2, 3, 4, 5, 6, 7 and 8, the likelihood is that you will finally have achieved your purpose of creating "new ideas that will satisfy some expressed or implied need of mankind". And to aid in insuring that such accomplishment is brought about with both ever-greater frequency and regularity, and ever-greater value, one more step is in order . . .

Step 9: Repeat the Process

This step should be interpreted and applied in two ways: (1) repeat the procedure relative to the particular problem at hand, to increase your chances of producing that much-wanted one-in-a-million idea; and (2) repeat the procedure for the purpose of developing the natural habit of thinking in this way.

Each of these meanings is "right", and each is important. As one who is primarily interested here and now in your *learning* most soundly, thoroughly and usefully about creativity, I regard the second as being of by far the greatest long-term importance, however, for it represents *the most effective single means of developing creative ability*.

Creative Thinking is largely a skill. By psychological definition, "A skill is a perfect habit." And the only way on earth to perfect any skill/habit is—practice, PRACTICE, PRACTICE.

X. NINE DEFINITE STEPS

Now, of course, you may not be quite satisfied with what has been said thus far about this PackCorp Scientific Approach to Creative Thinking. It is not quite complete enough, obviously. (Is *any* book ever *quite* complete?) And it may seem a bit too pat, a little too cut and dried. No doubt there are a number of questions still unanswered in your mind.

For one thing, you are probably wondering, "Must I really follow this procedure in definite, sequential, separate 'steps'?" My answer to such a question must be this:

In order fully to define and comprehend the process, it is necessary to break it down into separate steps, phases, operations, stages, functions. Which means that you actually should do, in this order . . .

1. *Pick a Problem*. Define the problem. Specify your objective.
2. *Get Knowledge*. Observe; explore; experiment. "Get the facts."
3. *Organize Knowledge*. Put your information in understandable form.
4. *Refine Knowledge*. Screen it for relationships and principles.
5. *Digest*. Let your conscious mind relax; put your subconscious to work.
6. *Produce Ideas*. *Ad lib,* or: Concentrate anew until ideas emerge.

7. *Re-work Ideas.* Check ideas for flaws. Re-work them; improve them.

8. *Put Ideas to Work.* Decide. Sell. Apply. Teach. Follow up.

9. *Repeat the Process*—until it becomes a natural habit.

. . . and—especially if you are comparatively new to CT in general—you should deliberately follow these nine steps in order.

But please note carefully: This should *not* be interpreted as inferring that any sort of stolid, sheep-like, slavish adherence to rigid ritual or "S.O.P." is in order! "Scientific" though this formula may be, it is so in the sense of being orderly, organized, thorough—not dogged, unimaginative or mechanical.

There not only is "room" for art in this formula. It is so structured as practically to *compel* free, imaginative, "artistic" consideration of problems.

Application of the PackCorp Scientific Approach (as of any other CT method or technique, for that matter) *must* be flexible, for a variety of reasons: Each step is so inter-related with the others as to defy clear delineation in many, if not most, instances. The mind tends to (and should) move tentatively through the steps, come to grips with the problem, test, re-trace, try another direction, skip exploringly, back-track, repeat, pause, and move forward again. Certain problems or circumstances may necessitate proceeding in somewhat spasmodic, start-and-stop fashion. Other situations may dictate *reversal* of procedure; as, for example, when one must do basic research (Get Knowledge) just to be able to *define* his problem(s). Occasionally, one may work for a considerable period of time on a given problem, only to find that many *sub*-problems must be solved before the main one can be tackled. And on rare, wonderful occasion, workable new ideas may leap to mind directly upon *stating* a problem (because, at some earlier period, significant information was stored away in the memory and lay dormant until this one "right" moment happened to come along).

The point is that the PakSA formula must be applied not in robot fashion, which produces only trite and hackneyed ideas, but flexibly, resourcefully—in its entirety—with special consideration of any special requirements of the particular problem or environment or situation with which one is dealing.

As a general rule, for initial practice, it is advisable to choose several comparatively simple problems, then to approach your first specific trials of the complete formula with a conscious, deliberate effort to apply it in strict 1-2-3 manner. This, better than anything else I know, will give you quick insight into "the nature of the beast". And this will also help to reveal how it can be made to work to best advantage on your particular problems—which, after all, is what is the most important consideration of all.

Action!

"Yes," perhaps you are thinking (this late?), "but what guarantee have I, not just that this so-called 'PackCorp Scientific Approach' works in some particular way, but that it will work for me at all?"

You have *no* such guarantee.

There is abundant evidence that creative people in virtually every field of human endeavor have followed essentially this same basic procedure in making their achievements. And our whole civilization is replete with developments that have come out of its application.

If you will forgive a personal-though-pertinent reference, this very book evolved from a deliberate, step-by-step application of PakSA.

But these—and any other examples I have given, or could give—are examples from the *past,* and pertain to *other* people.

Which, regardless of any personal preferences we might have, makes it inescapably clear: In *your* final, personal analysis, there is only one possible way for you to get a "guarantee" or "proof" of the efficacy of the PackCorp Scientific Approach to Creative Thinking, and that is—*try it for yourself.*

XI. SUMMARY—'PACKCORP SCIENTIFIC APPROACH' TO CREATIVE THINKING

Step 1: Pick a Problem.
Define the problem—in writing.

First, state what's wrong—what needs fixing.

Second, state your objective—what end-result you seek.

Step 2: Get Knowledge.

Get the known facts relevant to the problem. Get new knowledge. Study the written references on your subject. Experiment. Explore. Research deeply and broadly. Talk-with/question informed people. Check your findings, to avoid being misled. Put them in writing. Concentrate on getting information, not ideas, at this stage.

Step 3: Organize Knowledge.

Put your information into some sensible form.

Sort it. Classify it. Organize it.

Put it in writing.

Step 4: Refine Knowledge.

Screen your information for relationships and principles.

Match fact against fact; see what meanings they make together.

Look for similarities, differences, analogies, cause-and-effect, combinations—patterns—concepts—principles—ideas.

Step 5: Digest.

Remove the problem from your mind's "front burner" to its "back burner".

Let your conscious mind get a "second wind"; let your subconscious work on the problem.

Take up another problem, or relax, or work at a hobby, or enjoy some mild diversion—until refreshed.

Step 6: Produce Ideas—ad lib, or . . .

Concentrate anew on your problem until ideas begin to emerge.

As they occur, don't stop to judge them. Just produce them, and record them.

Build up as many alternatives as you can.

Step 7: Re-work Ideas.

Check your enthusiasm until you have checked your new ideas for flaws.

Examine each idea objectively. Question it; challenge it; improve it.

Step 8: Put Ideas to Work.

Decide which alternative ideas to put to work.

If the approval and acceptance of others are required, sell your ideas.

Plan each sale— decide the how/who/when/where in advance.

Allow enough time—don't try to rush or push.

Get participation—let others own a share so they'll help, not hinder.

Use "samples"—visualize each idea; show/demonstrate/illustrate.

Stress customer-interest—soft-pedal the "I"; stress the "You."

If new methods and skills are involved, teach them.

Step 9: Repeat the Process—until it becomes a natural habit.

XII. MINI-SUMMARY

Many people, I find, like the idea of having miniature printed summaries of CT-related material which can be kept on the person, ready for reference if and when needed.

On the hunch that you, too, might like this idea, I am providing you here with the means of making a card which summarizes some of the key points *re* the *Inhibitors of Creative Thinking* and the *PackCorp Scientific Approach to Creative Thinking*.

Inhibitors of Creative Thinking

1. POOR HEALTH—Physiological and psychological problems which interfere with ability to concentrate.
2. INADEQUATE MOTIVATION—Lack of desire to create.
3. MENTAL LAZINESS—Unwillingness to think.
4. LACK OF CURIOSITY—The inability to wonder.
5. SUPERFICIALITY—Shallowness and hastiness of thought.
6. REPRESSIVE TRAINING & EDUCATION—Early influences which discourage the exercise of natural curiosity. Educational practices which stress conformity, which teach how to imitate, not create.
7. JOB DEGRADATION—The relegation (including self-relega-

tion) of men to work that neither challenges, nor even permits use of, their mental capacities. The burdening of men with so much that is "urgent" that no time or energy is left for what is important. Over-fractionation and -simplification of jobs.

8. FAULTY OBSERVATION—Inability to see the obvious.

9. EMOTION-MINDEDNESS—The habit of permitting feelings to distort thinking and encumber reasoning processes.

10. JUDICIAL-MINDEDNESS—The tendency toward "reflex criticism"—automatic negative reaction to the new and different. Failure to appreciate that "Abilities wither under fault-finding, blossom under encouragement."

11. LABEL-MINDEDNESS—The habit of thinking from the basis of the names of things rather than the facts about them.

12. CONCEPTUAL BLOCKS—Mechanical habits of mind which channel thinking narrowly and fetter the imagination.

How to Create New Ideas

1. PICK A PROBLEM—Define your problem—in writing. State what's *wrong*—what needs fixing. State your *objective*—what end-result you seek.

2. GET KNOWLEDGE—Get known facts. Get new knowledge. Study written references. Experiment. Explore. Research deeply and broadly. Talk with informed people. Check your findings. Put them in writing.

3. ORGANIZE KNOWLEDGE—Put your information into understandable form. Sort it. Organize it. Write it.

4. REFINE KNOWLEDGE—Screen knowledge for *relationships* and *principles*. Match fact against fact. Look for similarities, differences, analogies, cause-and-effect, combinations, *patterns*. Apply "stimulator" questions. If new ideas still are slow in coming to mind . . .

5. DIGEST—Let the conscious mind get its "second wind". Put the subconscious to work. Relax, take up another problem, work at a hobby or enjoy some mild diversion—until refreshed. Then . . .

6. PRODUCE IDEAS—*ad lib*, or—Concentrate anew on your prob-

lem until ideas begin to emerge. As they occur, don't stop to judge them—produce them and write them. *Build up as many alternatives as you can.*

7. RE-WORK IDEAS—Check your new ideas for flaws. Examine each idea objectively—question it; challenge it; test it; re-work it; improve it; follow it through.

8. PUT IDEAS TO WORK—If the approval and acceptance of others are required, *sell* your ideas:

    Plan each sale. Allow enough time. Get participation. Use "samples". Stress *customer*-interest.

    If new methods and skills are involved, *teach* them.

9. REPEAT THE PROCESS—until it becomes a natural habit.

I. Thinker Toy #1

Cut out the pieces outlined below, then arrange them on a flat surface to form an *equilateral triangle*.

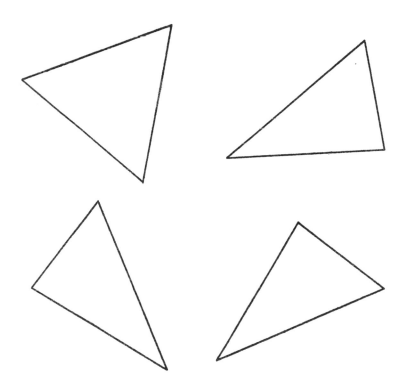

(Be careful not to damage other pages when cutting out these pieces.)

Seventh

HOW ABOUT SOME PRACTICE?

One of the main points made in the explanation of PakSA-CT was this:

Skill is developed through practice.

Another key point was this one:

Creative Thinking is basically a skill.

And a third point was this:

Games, problems, puzzles, etc. have great value as CT stimulators.

Combining and taking direction from these points . . .

Here, on the following pages, you will find a number of selected problems, "brain teasers," exercises, puzzles, "Thinker Toys" and projects. They are not intended to be used merely for entertainment—although I expect you'll get a lot of enjoyment from working with them—but are to help in stimulating your imagination and to provide practice to aid you in developing knowledgeable skill in making effective use of the principles, tools, methods and techniques of Creative Thinking.

Good CT'ing to you!

II. Names, Names, Names

Problem: Imagine that your company recently carried out a comprehensive program of training in Creative Thinking for every key man and woman in the organization. Now, the top executives want to follow up by instituting a formal *applied* CT program. In this follow-up program, however, the executives do not want to use the term, "creative thinking." (Some of the reasoning for this: Many people might associate the term with training rather than application. It can not be used with un-mistakable company identification as will be important in advertising, for example. And one executive even says that the term is itself "rather common and unimaginative.")

Objective: Think up an original, appealing term for CREATIVE THINKING.

   Tips:
   1. Use a thesaurus to "get the facts." Make up a list of synonyms for *"creative"* (original, productive, unique . . .), *"thinking"* (dreaming, cogitation, reasoning . . .) and related words.
   2. Search out pertinent principles—principles of phonetics, semantics, visual "impact," euphony, alliteration, psychological association and/or any others that might pertain.
   3. Try these approaches:
      a. Pairing of synonyms, as . . .
         Original Reasoning
         Practical Fantasy, etc.
      b. Coinage, as in joining portions of various "creative" words with part of the word *engineering* . . .
         Origineering
         Innoveering
         Visioneering, etc.
      c. Play on personal or company names, as . . .
         Gordonizing
         PackCogitation
         Autogenuity, etc.
      d. Play on initials or short "catch words," as . . .
         DO—Dynamic Origination
         AID—Avenue to Improvement Development
         IT, PIP, ACT . . . (You name them!)

III. THINKER TOY #2

Cut out the pieces outlined below, then arrange them on a flat surface to form *both* a *square* and a *triangle*.

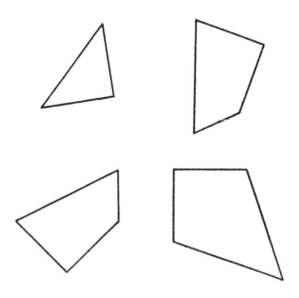

(Be careful not to damage other pages when cutting out these pieces.)

IV. Dovetails

How do you explain this?

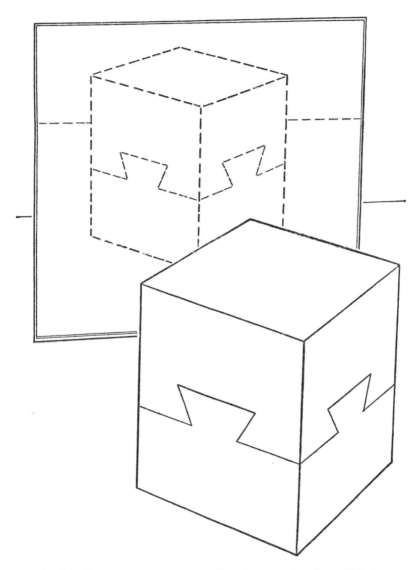

Indeed it *does* come apart—easily—in two simple, solid pieces.

V. THINKER TOY #3

Cut out the pieces outlined below, then arrange them on a flat surface to form a regular *hexagon*.

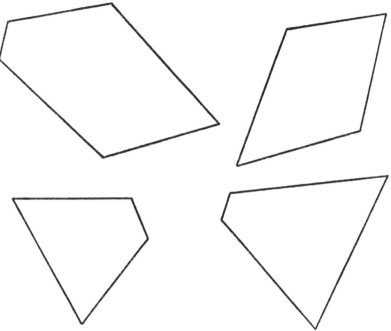

(Be careful not to damage other pages when cutting out these pieces.)

VI. BR-R-R!

Problem: Imagine that it is a sub-zero Saturday night in January, and a boy has just thrown a snowball through a small window in your kitchen. The snowball knocked out all the glass in the window-opening—which is a square one, 12" by 12". All stores are closed, so it is impossible for you to get a new window pane now. Meanwhile, it is terribly cold and blustery outside, and the cold wind is blasting into your house. In searching for something with which to close the window-opening until you can get a new pane on Monday, the only possibly applicable materials you can find are (1) a 27-inch length of two-inch-wide gummed tape, and (2) a rectangular piece of fiberboard, 9" x 16".

Objective: Cut the 9" x 16" piece of fiberboard into TWO pieces which, when fitted together and taped, will form a solid 12" x 12" square that can be used to seal the window-opening.

VII. THINKER TOY #4

Cut out the pieces outlined below, then arrange them on a flat surface to form a *square*.

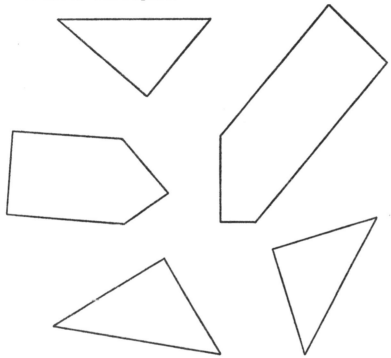

(Be careful not to damage other pages when cutting out these pieces.)

VIII. ALICE' MALICE

Problem: Imagine that your friend Alice sent you a piece of beautiful, random-patterned fabric from Europe, while touring, and that she also suggested that you use the fabric to make the tapestry you have always wanted for your living-room wall. Unfortunately, however, the piece of fabric Alice sent (maliciously?)

is a *rectangular* one—two feet wide by ten feet long—whereas, for proper artistic balance, your tapestry should be *square*.

Objective: Cut the 2′ x 10′ piece into FIVE pieces that can be sewed together to form a perfect square, without waste.

IX. Thinker Toy #5

Cut out the pieces outlined below, then arrange them on a flat surface to form a regular *pentagon*.

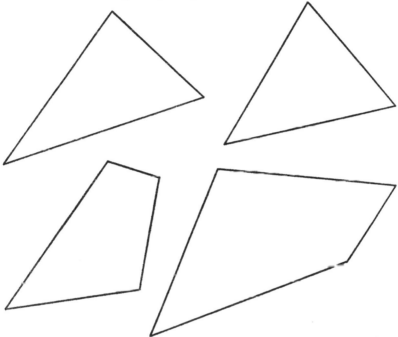

(Be careful not to damage other pages when cutting out these pieces.)

X. "Material X" Again

Problem: A well-known company in the paper industry has developed a new machine-made product, a sketch of which you see here . . .

This product is made up of (1) paper—folded, as you see; (2) a ribbon of textile filaments; and (3) an adhesive. Each of these component materials is somewhat variable—*e.g.*, the paper can be of practically any type, etc., *a la* "Material X"; the ribbon/filaments could be of natural or synthetic fiber, or of metal, glass, etc.; and the adhesive might be any of a number of different kinds. The size of the product is variable, too; and it can be made in virtually any length. But (and here is the essence of the problem) as yet, no one has developed any appreciable number of *uses* for this product.

Objective: Develop all the uses you can for this product.

XI. THINKER TOY #6

Cut out the piece outlined below, then divide it into *four congruent pieces*.

(Be careful not to damage other pages when cutting out this piece.)

XII. NEW MATERIAL

One of the most flagrant examples of Label-Mindedness—and resultant wastefulness—is our (lazy-minded?) habit of identifying certain materials as "waste" or "scrap," *period*. To our great

advantage, we ought to pledge ourselves *not* to use these labels, but instead to say to ourselves, "Here we have some materials with certain qualities—materials for which there may be a great many uses, such as . . ."

"Mere whimsy," you say? Pulp by-products are utilized further to improve plastics, soap, paper, rubber, paint. Grain hulls and corncobs are used in making nylon. Coke-oven gas is recovered and put to use in the manufacture of dyes, perfumes, vitamins. *Not* so whimsical!

Operation New-Material:

List every material which you have been in the habit of mislabeling, as above. Then—go ahead and do what you already know you should do.

XIII. THINKER TOY #7

Cut out the piece outlined below, then divide it into *four congruent pieces.*

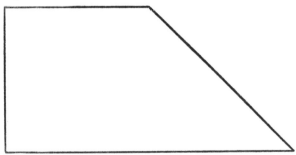

(Be careful not to damage other pages when cutting out this piece.)

XIV. IDIOMIDIOCIES

A great deal that is passed around as being "good, solid horse sense" would be an insult to the dullest old swayback. A sample . . .

"He never met a payroll."
"I could buy and sell him ten times over."
"He can't amount to much—why, I grew up with the guy!"

Horse-sense lovers of the world, arise against this awful blight! Haul out those moldy, old, idiotic idioms—or idiomatic idiocies, as the case may be—haul them out into the light of day, and expose them to the twist of truth. Like so . . .

Old: "If he's so smart, why ain't he rich?"
New: "If he's so rich, why ain't he smart?" (Continue...)

Old: _____
New: _____

Old: _____
New: _____

Old: _____
New: _____

XV. THINKER TOY #8

Cut out the pieces outlined below, then arrange them on a flat surface to form a *square*.

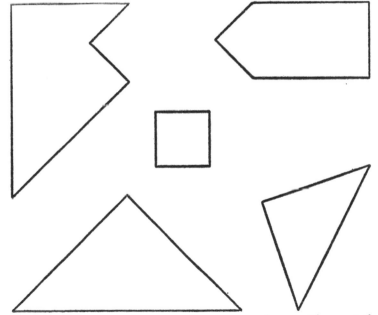

(Be careful not to damage other pages when cutting out these pieces.)

XVI. T.N.T.—Ten Noggin Twisters

1. If a pencil and an eraser cost $1.10, and the pencil cost $1.00 more than the eraser, how much did the eraser cost?

2. Arrange the letters, "C-H-E-S-T-Y," to spell another English word. (They will spell only one word other than "chesty.")

3. If a roof peak runs east and west, and the rooster on the peak faces south, which way will the egg roll?

4. Selecting them in the dark from a drawer containing 10 gray socks and 10 blue socks mixed together, how many socks would you have to choose to be sure of getting a matched pair?

5. If one brick weighs ¾ of a pound and ¾ of a brick, what is the weight of two bricks?

6. A phonograph record is 12 inches in diameter. At its outer edge is an unrecorded band ½ inch in width; the unrecorded center circle is 5 inches in diameter; in the recorded band, there are 100 grooves to the inch. How far does the needle travel when the record is played?

7. If a hen and a half laid an egg and a half in a day and a half, how long would it take the hen to day a dozen eggs?

8. If a father bull weighs 2,000 pounds, and a mother bull weighs 1,500 pounds, what will their baby bull weigh?

9. When I am as old as my father is now, I will be five times as old as my son is now. By then my son will be 8 years younger than I am now. Combined age of my father and myself is 100 years. Hold old is my son?

10. Make eight 8's equal 1,000.

XVII. Thinker Toy #9

Cut out the pieces outlined next, then arrange them on a flat surface to form *a regular block-style letter of the English alphabet*. (Yes, *you* have to determine *which* letter of the alphabet can be formed with these pieces. That shouldn't be too difficult, however; for, as you can see, none of the pieces has any

curved lines, which therefore rules out the possibility that the letter in question could be B, C, D, G, J, O, P, Q, R, S, or U.)

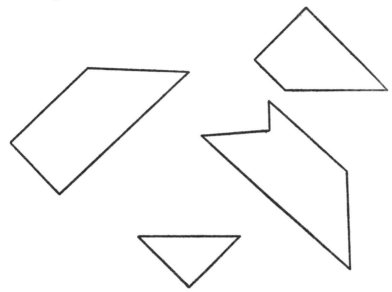

(Be careful not to damage other pages when cutting out these pieces.)

XVIII. ONEDERFUL JUORDS ("WONDERFUL WORDS")

One evening during a longer-than-usual business visit in New York, and tired of the customary hotel-dining-room fare, I walked over a good part of mid-town Manhattan in search of an out-of-the-way, "different" dining place. I had little success, though, and was about to give up, just off Times Square, when suddenly I saw a small sign in a restaurant window . . .

BEST GHOTI DINNER IN THE CITY

"*Ghoti*"? Naturally, I went in. A waiter greeted me: "*Fish—* '*GH*' as in '*rough*,' '*O*' as in '*women*,' and '*TI*' as in '*position*.'" Can *you* think of any other ways of spelling "fish"?

*   *   *

In his fine book on problem-solving, Edward Hodnett avers

that the letters of the words, "DRY OXTAIL IN REAR," can be arranged to form *one* English word. What word is it?

* * *

Richard Allen took his speech-classmates' minds entirely off the subject of speech with the question, "What common English word has three sets of double letters?" Do you know to what word he referred?

* * *

What other "worddities" do you know, or can you think up— and how can they be used?

* * *

XIX. VEE-VEE

In the literature of business and industry, these days, it seems there is a popular and recurring treatment of the subject of "Communication." And, in this treatment, there appears to be a standard exhortation to *"Write as you speak!"*

Can you imagine what would happen, though, if we really, *literally* did as exhorted?

A Texan would write, *"Thetsuh fur peese,"* for "That is a considerable distance." An Ohioan might make it, *"Gnaw splay gnat,"* rather than "Now, explain that." A New Jerseyite would record, *"Yoozul roonut inna wurtr,"* not, "You will ruin it in the water." A Maine Yankee could jot down, *"Paaquia caantha baan,"* when he intended the directive, "Park your car in the barn." A Tennesseean would write, *"Ih himme nantams rat owna hay ed,"* meaning—believe it or not!—"It hit me nine times, right on the head."

And almost any two Americans might exchange the correspondence . . . *"Jeet jet?"* *"Know Jew?"* . . . meaning: "Did you eat yet?" "No. Did you?"

Now, the object of these colloquial calisthenics is not merely to have phun with phonics (although it might be riotous to translate The Gettysburg Address into Brooklynese, for example). Rather, it is to present a curious, human phenomenon for possible creative *application*.

So . . .

First: How about a *name?* Say, "Visual Vernacular," "Vee-Vee," or "VV"? Or: _____

_____

_____

_____

Second: How about some *uses* for VV? Say, in military code. (Can you picture the consternation of a Soviet interpreter, trying to decipher the VV of a 'Bama boy?) Or: _____

_____

_____

_____

_____

_____

_____

_____

_____

_____

_____

_____

_____

_____

_____

_____

_____

_____

XX. FOR KEEPS

1. Devise ten new ways to save money in your business.
2. List your boss's problems, then work out solutions for each one.
3. Name your "pet peeve," then figure out how it might be alleviated.
4. Describe the best idea you have ever had, then list 10 benefits to be gained from its adoption.
5. Suppose someone gave you 10,000 typewriter-ribbon spools. What uses can you devise for them?
6. Identify five faults which bother you, impede your progress, or lessen your effectiveness. Then develop a plan for correcting them.

7. Choose an object from your home or place of business, and figure out an improved container or package for it.
8. Recall the last time you lost your temper. State what you gained by it and what you lost. Develop a plan for regaining what you lost.
9. Imagine that you were suddenly selected to succeed your boss's boss. Specify the changes you would make—and why.
10. Describe the problem that bothers you most in life. Then list ten ways of coping with it.

XXI. Culmination

If you are really, deeply, dedicatedly burning with eager determination to undertake the creative solution of "something to get the teeth into," you could hardly choose anything of greater desirability and potential benefit to humanity than . . .

One

Problem: There is conflict in the world.
Objective: Create peace.

Two

Problem: In the face of great human need, there is the fact that about two tenths of one percent of the energy of the sunshine that comes to earth, if collected, controlled and directed in certain ways, could just about double our supply of food—and everything else we use.
Objective: Capture and apply this sunshine.

* * *

These "two" problems may actually be one and the same.

* * *

Eighth

IS THERE OTHER 'CT' READING

MATTER?

In all truth, I know of very little reading matter that does *not* pertain somewhat and somehow to the subject of Creative Thinking. For, excepting only cheap fiction and similar trash, virtually *anything* that one reads may supply either raw-material/information for idea building, or additional insight into the nature of man and his thinking—both of which are not only pertinent, but invaluable. If required to be more specific, however, I would—and do—especially recommend these 50 publications:

Professional Creativity, Von Fange; Prentice-Hall, Inc.
The Sources of Invention, Jewkes *et al;* St. Martin's Press.
Creativity and Its Cultivation, Anderson *et al;* Harper & Brothers.
Imagination, Undeveloped Resource, Cros, Gamble, Mraz & Whiting Assoc's.
Ingenuity, Kogan; Creative Thinking Institute.
The Techniques of Creative Thinking, Crawford; Hawthorn Books, Inc.
Instruction in Creative Mechanical Design, DuBois; ASME Paper 53-A-172.
The Creative Process, Von Fange; General Electric Company.
How to Produce New Ideas, Garrison; Popular Mechanics.
Applied Imagination, Osborn; Charles Scribner's Sons.
Power of Words, Chase; Harcourt, Brace & Company.

The Nature of Creative Thinking; Industrial Research Institute, Inc.

Finding the Range; Creative Thinking Institute.

Creative and Mental Growth, Lowenfeld; Macmillan, N. Y.

The Creative Process, Ghiselin; University of California Press.

Improving the Perfect; Creative Thinking Institute.

Hold It Up by Gravity; Creative Thinking Institute.

Looking Ahead; Creative Thinking Institute.

Essentials in Problem Solving; Creative Thinking Institute.

The Art of Clear Thinking, Flesch; Harper & Brothers.

Thinking Straight, Beardsley; Prentice-Hall, Inc.

Creativity, Guilford; American Psychologist.

Cognitive, Creative and Non-Intellective Intelligence, Wechsler; Am. Psych.

How to Develop Your Thinking Ability, Keyes; McGraw-Hill Book Company.

The Technique of Getting Things Done, Laird(s); Whittlesey House.

A Technique for Producing Ideas, Young; Advertising Publications.

The Mature Mind, Overstreet; W. W. Norton & Co., Inc.

How to Think Creatively, Hutchinson; Abingdon-Cokesbury, N. Y.

Directed Thinking, Humphrey; Dodd, Mead & Company, Inc.

Logic for Millions, Mander; Philosophical Library.

Twelve Rules for Straight Thinking, Reilly; Harper & Brothers.

Critical Thinking, Black; Prentice-Hall, Inc.

Right Thinking, Burtt; Harper & Brothers.

On Problem Solving, Duncker; American Psychological Association.

Productive Thinking, Wertheimer; Harper & Brothers.

How to Solve It, Polya; Princeton University Press.

An Experiment in the Development of Critical Thinking, Glaser; Colum. Un.

How to Get Original Ideas, Wortley; Park Row Pub. House.

The Rhyme of Reason, Holmes; D. Appleton-Century Co., Inc.

Thinking to Some Purpose, Stebbing; Penguin Books.

The Art of Straight Thinking, Clark; D. Appleton-Century
   Co., Inc.

How to Think Straight, Thouless; Simon & Schuster, Inc.

Education and the Psychology of Thinking, Symonds; Mc-
   Graw-Hill Book Co.

How to Think Clearly, Jepson; Longmans, Green & Co., Inc.

The Habit of Scientific Thinking: A Handbook for Teachers;
   Columbia Univ.

How to Think, Dewey; D. C. Heath & Co.

Reason and Nature, Cohen; Harcourt, Brace & Co., Inc.

Ideas, Husserl; The Macmillan Company.

The Art of Thinking, Dimnet; Simon & Schuster, Inc.

How to Think in Business, McClure; McGraw-Hill Book Company.

Ninth

WHAT HAVE THOUGHTFUL
THINKERS THOUGHT?

When I first started gathering materials for this book, I got together a collection of profound statements by deep thinkers, with a kind of partially-thought-out intention of sprinkling them around through the book in somewhat the same style employed by many scholarly writers. And then, to be honest about it, I had one blankety-blank of a time trying to fit them into the book in some related, makes-sense, appropriate way. Whereupon —finally!—I started thinking:

Why should these quotations be scattered about like the leaves of autumn or the beads off a broken strand? What difference will it make to *you*, the reader? What use, if any, will you make of these statements? In a book on creativity (of *all* places!) isn't it just about totally inexcusable to imitate other authors for no other real reason than merely to imitate other authors? And so on.

The upshot, as you see, was that I decided to put all these pearls together for you on one string. Like so . . .

Thoughtful Thinkers' Thoughts on Thinking

Everybody is ignorant, only on different subjects.
—Will Rogers

The greatest achievements of mankind have been accomplished by two types of people—those who were smart enough to know it could be done, and those too dumb to know it couldn't.
—Dunno

Few minds wear out—more rust out.

—Bovee

The reasonable man adapts himself to the world. The unreasonable man persists in trying to adapt the world to himself. Therefore all progress depends upon the unreasonable man.

—Shaw

Chance favors only minds which are prepared.

—Pasteur

The big ideas in this world can not survive unless they come to life in the individual citizen. It is what each man does in responding to his convictions that provides the great forward thrust for any great movement.

—Cousins

I have never let my schooling interfere with my education.

—Twain

The blessed work of helping the world forward does not wait to be done by perfect men.

—Dunno

An educated man is one on whom nothing is lost.

—Wendell Smith

Criticism is something we can avoid easily—by saying nothing, doing nothing and being nothing.

—Dunno

Research is nothing but a state of mind—a friendly, welcoming attitude toward change; going out to look for a change instead of waiting for it to come . . . Research, for practical men, is an effort to do things better . . . The research state of mind can apply to anything—personal affairs, or any kind of business, big or little.

—Kettering

If you itch for something, scratch for it.

—Dunno

Real knowledge, like everything else of the highest value, is not to be obtained easily. It must be worked for, studied for, thought for; and, more than all, it must be prayed for.

—Thomas Arnold

The failure of many to succeed is due more to lack of will power than to lack of brain power.

—Dunno

There is room at the top—but it is no rest room.

—Dunno

Many ideas grow better when transplanted into another mind than the one where they sprang up.

—Holmes

When you stop to think, don't forget to start again.

—Dunno

Research is an organized method of finding out what you are going to do when you can't keep on doing what you are doing now.

—Kettering

Unexpected weaknesses, wherever and whenever they emerge, can be traced to a *rushed* job.

—Dunno

One who fears failure limits his worth. Failure is only the opportunity to begin again more intelligently.

—Henry Ford

To rest content with results achieved is the first sign of decay.

—Dunno

A determined soul will do more with a rusty monkey wrench than a loafer will accomplish with all the tools in the machine shop.

—Hughes

Just the moment you get satisfied with what you have accomplished, the concrete has begun to harden in your head.

—Kettering

The only thing that will overcome a persuasive idea is a better one.

—Repplier

The ability to generalize accurately is almost priceless. Most people go to one or the other extreme: (1) they never draw any conclusions at all from the world of observable fact, or (2) they draw wildly incorrect conclusions from next-to-no data.

—Rogers, Slade and Hill

Thinking, not mere physical growth, makes manhood.

—Isaac Taylor

Reaction to new ideas usually passes through these stages:

1. Crazy! How silly can you be?

   2. These ideas are dangerous. They must be vigorously
       opposed.
   3. Why, of course! Who ever thought otherwise?

—Alvin Hansen

The opportunities in this world are as great as we have imagination to see them; but we never get the view from the bottom
of a rut.

—Kettering

There are four steps in achievement:
   1. Decide.
   2. Start.
   3. Stick.
   4. Finish.

—Dunno

Tenth

HAS SOMETHING BEEN
OVERLOOKED?

"Overlooked?" Not exactly. Deferred, really. And the principal matter so deferred has been that of giving recognition and credit where due.

There is a simple-enough explanation as to why this matter has been put off as long as possible: I must now directly face the truth—the embarrassing, uncomfortable truth—that I don't really *know* the depth and extent of my indebtedness. Oh, surely—I "know," in a fuzzy way, that certain concepts, insights, points of view, illustrations, twists, knowledges, philosophies, etc. likely originated with someone else (at least embryonically); and I have probably only changed them enough, and waited long enough, to have obscured their specific origin. Too, much of what I have proffered here with a proprietary air, however unwittingly, no doubt is actually such a merging/distillation/alloy/mutation/amorphous-blend of impressions, teachings, mullings, analyses, gleanings, gifts, conclusions, etc., *ad infinitum* as absolutely to defy any attempt at tracing lineage. And, of course, there is the now-disquieting realization that I have made very little *effort* to take note of where things came from; but have just kept going along insensately, all the while, about like the fellow idly considering the possible purchase of a new car: "I don't care who invented the first one—I just want to know which is the *best* one."

But, even if this explains my dereliction, it hardly meets my obligation, does it? So, however incompletely, I here and now

221

do publicly declare my gratitude and appreciation to many, many creative benefactors—including:

Blanche Jones	Helen Harper	Raymond Getty
Rebecca Barrick	Clyde Justice	Steele Swope
Eddie Connors	Creighton Hoopes	Paul Crispin
Joseph Hummel	Walter James	Sam Greene
Hamilton Herritt	Walter Jamouneau	David Long
Joseph McElwee	Emilio Frasca	Fred Crandall
Richard Stotler	Harry Hibler	Harold Moss
James Anderson	James Foster	Vladimir Krumhansl
Maxine Zivick	Walter Dmytryk	Alan MacCurdy
Marjory Rohrer	Helen Van Gilder	John Sigrist
Robert Hildenbrand	Lewis Burnett	William Creson
Martin Cipar	Carl Romack	John Delagrange
Fred Hartman	James Higgins	John Zivick
Alvin Simberg	George Contogeorgis	Dorothy Parr
Burton Teague	Richard Schweitzer	Charles Kalb
William Westberg	Muriel Merkel	Eugene Harris
Ernest Scott	Ordway Tead	Homer Castor
Jane Taylor	Margaret Bowman	Arnold Greene
John Staley	Edith Lynch	Paul Ebert
Richard Guyton	Fred Somma	Donald Effler
William Schopf	Howard Sigmond	Gerald Galbo

. . . plus hundreds upon hundreds of the people of the Packaging Corporation of America, its supervisors, managers and executives (Mr. Hall and Mr. Prentice say, "Space . . .")—and my beloved "EBT" and Dad and Mother, whom I could never honor enough.

Oh, Yes—Regarding "SEVENTH: HOW ABOUT SOME PRACTICE?" . . .

I. Thinker Toy #1:

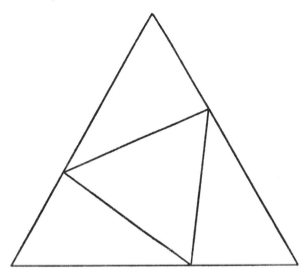

II. Names, Names, Names:
Any answer that meets the objective is a "right" answer.

III. Thinker Toy #2:

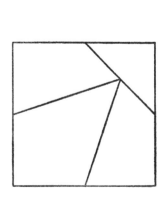
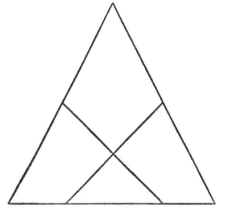

IV . Dovetails:

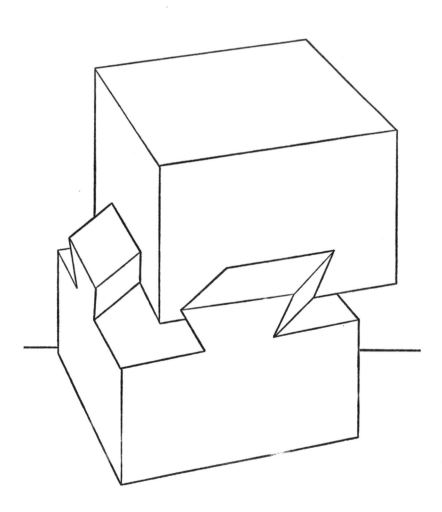

V. Thinker Toy #3:

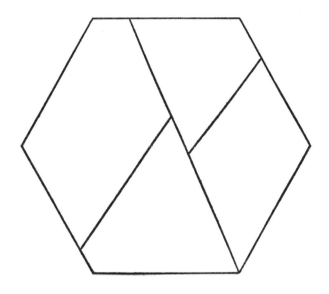

VI. Br-r-r!:
   Cut the rectangle . . .

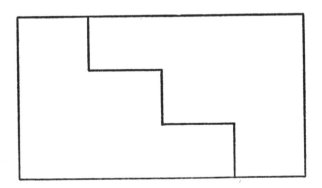

Make the square . . .

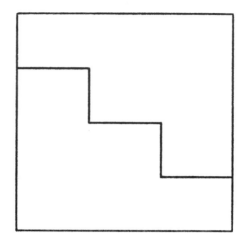

VII.   Thinker Toy #4:

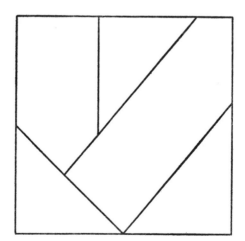

VIII. Alice' Malice:
Cut the rectangle . . .

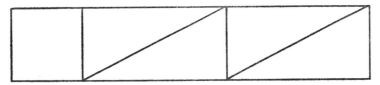

Make the square . . .

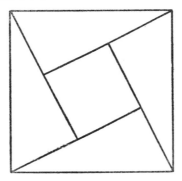

IX. Thinker Toy #5:

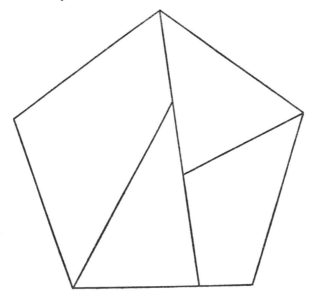

X. "Material X" Again:

The probability is that *every one* of your ideas here is a "right" one. More important, though, is this:

Which ones are you going to follow through and develop into final, practicable form?

Which ones are you going to carry beyond the stage of being mere "interesting possibilities"?

Which ones are you finally going to put into constructive *use?*

XI. Thinker Toy #6:

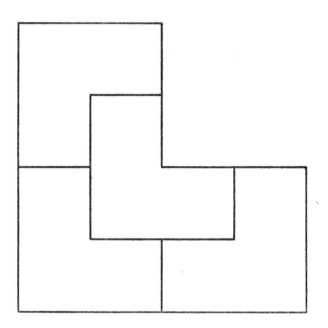

XII. New Material:

No comment—because no comment is needed.

XIII. Thinker Toy #7:

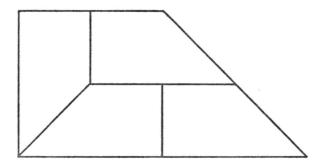

XIV. Idiomidiocies:
If you got *any* answer, that's progress!

XV. Thinker Toy #8:

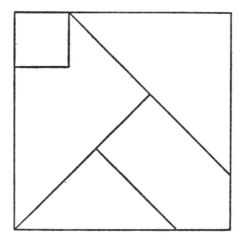

XVI. T.N.T.—Ten Noggin Twisters:

1. $.05.
2. Scythe.
3. This depends on how one defines "rooster," hmm?
4. Three.
5. Six pounds.
6. The needle will travel the three-inch width of the recorded band.
7. Eighteen days.
8. There is no such thing as a "mother bull."
9. Twelve years.
10. 888
    88
     8
     8
    ———
    1000

XVII. Thinker Toy #9:

XVIII. Onederful Juords:
   1. "DRY OXTAIL IN REAR"—*extraordinarily.*
   2. "English word . . . three sets of double letters"—*bookkeeper.*

XIX. Vee-Vee:
   No "right" or "wrong" here. Just good, better and best.

XXI. For Keeps—and—XXII. Culmination:
   I wish you the greatest possible success with these!

Eleventh

SO?

Robert Crawford, one of America's most respected students and teachers of Creative Thinking, has said,

> *"Three things move the world:*
> *IDEAS,*
> plus
> *MAKING THEM WORK,*
> plus
> *MAKING OTHERS LIKE THEM."* [1]

A very great deal remains to be learned about creativity—what it is, how it works, how to work it. But there is every reason to believe that with what *is* currently known—specifically as exemplified in the principles, methods, tools and techniques presented in this book—*you* can "move the world" forward. There is just one question:

When do you plan to start?

---

[1] From *The Techniques of Creative Thinking,* by Robert P. Crawford. Copyright 1954 by Hawthorn Books, Inc., 70 Fifth Avenue, New York, N. Y. Published by Hawthorn Books, Inc.

INDEX

INDEX

A

Abilities, flourish under encouragement, 33
Acceptance of ideas, securing, 175-177
Adler, Alfred, 164
Alcohol, inhibits creative activity, 166
Alternatives, deciding between, 172-175
  intuitive approach, 173
  known-odds approach, 174
  ranking approach, 173-174
  saturation approach, 173
  statistical-analysis approach, 174-175
Amateurs:
  breakthroughs in science made by, 65
  inventions by, 64-66
American Psychological Association, 10
Applied Imagination (Osborn), 49, 157
Approval of ideas, securing, 175-177
Arthur D. Little, Incorporated, 55
  Gordon Technique used by, 55-56
Atom bomb, 63
Atomic Energy Commission, 64
Attribute listing, 66-69
  evaluation of ideas, 69
  features of, 67-69
  objective, 108
  practice exercises, 68-69
  procedure, 67-69
  technique of creative thinking, 66
  used for improving tangible things, 66
Authorship, principle of, 161
Aviation, solving problem of, 151

B

Batten, Barton, Durstine & Osborn, 49
Berlioz, Louis H., 167-168
Bibliography, 214-216
Biro Brothers, 14
Brain:
  analytical function, 4
  electronic brain compared to human, 8

Brain (*cont.*)
  imaginer or "thinker-upper," 4
  nervous energy consumed by, 17
  nervous system and, 7-8
  restored by food and rest, 18
  retainer functions of, 3
  strengthened by exercise, 18
  "thinking" capacity of, 8
  weight of, 3
Brainstorming, 49-51, 107-108
  developed by Alex Osborn, 49
  disadvantages, 52-54
  evaluation of group's suggestions, 50
  experimental sessions, 51-52
  formation of group, 49-50
  "free-wheeling," nature of, 50, 52-53
  ground rules, 50
  group approach, 53
  limitations on use of, 52-54
  objective, 108
  quantity of ideas wanted, 50
  suggested exercises, 54-55
  techniques, 50-51
  uninhibited conference-type group approach, 50, 54
Brain teasers, value of, 159, 189-213
Breakthroughs in science, made by amateurs, 65

C

California Institute of Technology, 98
Campbell, John, 64-65
Catalog techniques for creating new ideas, 72-75, 109
  adaptations and modifications of existing ideas, 74
  catalogs as a means of getting new ideas, 73
  procedure, 73-75
  using present ideas in the development of new ideas, 74
Change, importance of, 165
Check-list technique of creative thinking, 88-97, 110
  features of, 88-95
  package-planning, 89-95
  possible-solution ("P-S") list, 89,

235

71

1